THE
BOTTOM
LINE

How to Build
a Business
Case for

ISO 14001

THE BOTTOM LINE

How to Build a Business Case for
ISO 14001

PAM PARRY

S^t_L

St. Lucie Press
Boca Raton   London   New York   Washington, D.C.

Library of Congress Cataloging-in-Publication Data

Parry, Pam (Pamela Ann)
     The bottom line : how to build a business case for ISP 14001 / Pam
Parry ; foreword by Mary C. McKiel.
             p.   cm.
       ISBN 1-57444-249-X (alk. paper)
         1. ISO 14000 Series Standards. 2. Production management–
     –Environmental aspects. 3. Environmental management—Standards.
     I. Title.
     TS155.7.P37 1999
     658.4'08—dc21   99-40302
                                                                                            CIP

© 2000 by CRC Press LLC
St. Lucie Press is an imprint of CRC Press LLC

No claim to original U.S. Government works
International Standard Book Number 1-57444-249-X
Library of Congress Card Number   99-40302
Printed in the United States of America   1 2 3 4 5 6 7 8 9 0
Printed on acid-free paper

Dedication

For my parents, Myron and Ann Parry, and my brothers and sister, Mike, Bob, Jim, and Sue, who have given me a lifetime of love and support.

Dedication

Contents

Foreword

"Batter my heart, three-personed God; for You
As yet but knock, breathe, shine, and seek to mend;
That I may rise and stand, o'erthrow me, and bend
Your force to break, blow, burn, and make me new."

— John Donne
Sonnet 14

Notes of an ISO 14000 Watcher

Change is not good. All things biological and physical resist it. Even when we humans desire the outcome of a change, our nature prefers the status quo unless acted on by sufficient motivation. We're particularly resistant to changes forced on us or not of our own making. Good is a value-laden notion, but considering that the universe is constantly changing, one might expect the overall stress level to be, well, pangalactic in proportion. Fortunately, there's an almost infinite variety of coping mechanisms and, thankfully, not all change occurs rapidly.

John Donne's plea is to be changed in the face of his own massive and self-perceived intractable nature. Although taken out of context here, the message is not without genuine applicability. Donne recognizes that it is going to take forceful, directed efforts to crack through his hardened heart to find fulfillment, wisdom, and truth and that he can't do it by himself. The good he seeks is intensely personal, but not necessarily solitary in effect.

In preparing to write this foreword to a book on ISO 14001, I found myself at the doorstep of Donne. Whatever changes may be possible through the use of 14001, whatever changes are already occurring, perceiving the truth of what the changes are and mean requires intellectual honesty and emotional malleability. Like Donne, I believe these come about through intense effort, well-directed communication, and interaction with outside forces.

Lewis Thomas' book "Lives of a Cell"[1] continues to be a fount of inspiration. Referring to himself as a biology watcher, Thomas traverses the microscopic world, pausing to muse on some of its biggest tiny secrets, and then with seamless ease transports the reader to a perch somewhere above the cosmos to consider how even the smallest mysteries interconnect to form the pattern of our universe, our lives, and our relationships.

Thomas' eloquent approach may not work perfectly in musings on ISO 14001 but I believe in "interconnectedness." Nothing in the biological, physical, spiritual, economic, or social world points toward complete isolation as a preferred mode for long-term existence. Neither is any event grasped in totality without consideration of connectedness whether it's something as small as intercellular activity or as moderately sized as implementing an ISO 14001-based system. To make those connections, we need information derived from data, facts, hearsay, feelings, technical and historical perspectives plus many other sources and, finally, a reliable crystal ball. The mighty trick is keeping these straight and, with Donne, forcing our biases to be broken and burned and removed in order to see the truth.

Every serious researcher does daily mortal combat with the dragons of his or her own predisposition or biases. The second worse nightmare is to find that "the numbers" reflect an initial bias rather than unfold a truth. The worse nightmare is that someone else discovered this before you did. Science and philosophy have never been that far apart. Philosophers ask: How can I be certain that I know what I know? Physicist Heisenberg preempted the question with his Uncertainty Principle, stating that the very observation of the physical phenomena changes the phenomena.

When it comes to ISO 14001 and EMS, what do we know and how do we know it? Here's one way to look at it. About 94 million years ago, the super continent of Pangaea began to break up, rifting into three parts: Eurasia-North America, Africa-South America, and Antarctica-Australia-India. Pangaea's breakup took about 44 million years and then a new cycle of continental collisions began. Africa hit Europe, and India rammed into Asia, thrusting up the Alps and Himalayas. Continental compression led to widened ocean basins, which lowered sea levels. Migration routes emerged and land animals flourished. Fifty million years later, ISO 14001 was published.

Well, this is a fact and gives us some sense of connectedness, but it's difficult to assess real meaning. Getting to meaningful comprehension is not easy, nor does it follow a single path.

In the United States, the Multi-State Working Group (MSWG) on ISO 14001 and the U.S. Environmental Protection Agency (EPA) seem to lead the pack of those who are testing and evaluating the use of EMS and the ISO standard. Other groups are interested as well — certainly environmental organizations — but the bulk of the pilot projects and data gathering is probably being done by the EPA and the MSWG. Both the EPA and the MSWG already have made explicit connectedness of ISO 14001 to regulatory actions, albeit from different viewpoints at times. Federal and state regulators by virtue of their public roles must think along public policy lines as they progress through the EMS and ISO 14001 woods.

Industry in the United States (and by this I exclude consultants, representatives of standards organizations, private sector not-for-profit groups, and a host of others) is not, generally speaking, engaged in testing out EMS and ISO 14001. Instead, the decision to build an EMS and to use the ISO standard to do so, requires business-thinking and analysis. The decision to become certified is linked but separate. A variety of periodicals and publications, including CEEM'S *International Environmental Systems Update*, regularly update the tally on who's getting certified to ISO.[2] Suffice it to say that even when a company is motivated by improvement for environment and adherence to laws and regulations, the value of 14001 is essentially a business value.

Environmental groups bridge industry and government on behalf of the public, vigilant for signs that environmental protection measures may be in danger due to actions of the other two sectors. Environmental organizations give mixed reviews at best to the use of ISO 14001 either in the public policy arena or as a credible basis for communicating performance to the general public.

The value system of each group is different ... related, certainly, but different. The question is: Which one has the right answers? At this point, let me make it perfectly clear that my remarks are my remarks and do not necessarily represent any of the views of my agency. The EPA has issued an official EMS/ISO 14001 policy statement, which is included as Appendix B of this book. If a reader is interested in policies of the agency, they are not being forged in these pages. If anything here is somehow contrary to a policy of the agency, stick with the agency, knowing that I've erred. Now, having set that straight, we're back to the questions: Who knows what is right? and Who knows how to know?

For my part, I confess: I believe they are all right, but time will tell. David Schnare in his chapter on "Stewardship Ethic" in the *Handbook for Environmental Risk Decision Making*, addresses what he sees as a critical framework for environmentalists in drawing conclusions related to risk assessment. "The most important element ... leading to the environmentalist's dilemma is that the conflict is a disagreement between humans about the value of things from the human perspective. This dilemma is of human construction — not because of human actions, but because of human interests and values."[3]

The passage may well apply to each of the different entities attempting to produce information and draw conclusions from the implementation of ISO 14001 and EMS. One thing that ISO 14001 is not is a panacea for anyone. It cannot be applied like a Band-Aid to rectify public policy shortcomings or shore-up gaps in performance or lull environmentalists into complacency. Whatever values and motivations drive the use of ISO 14001, it will fail in all respects if the users and evaluators are content that "by dreaming of systems so perfect that no one will need to be good."[4]

Understanding what ISO 14001 has to offer to various groups requires a discipline of information, a sense of connectedness, and an open heart. It's relatively easy to generate data and it's very easy to generate data to say what the generator wants to conclude. Not a Ph.D. student in the world, I dare say, would find a quarrel with this and would recognize it for the horrible temptation that it is.

Speaking of the difficulties in knowing the truth of our human origins, G.A. Clark squared off two conflicting but accepted models for development. Both models provide mathematically and aesthetically engaging data and conclusions, but they are incompatible. Clark's warning as to the danger of this situation might be applied to the quest for truth surrounding ISO 14001.

He said: "... we select among alternative sets of [one another's] research conclusions in accordance with our biases and preconceptions. These biases and preconceptions must be subjected to critical scrutiny. As long as there is no explicit concern with the logic of inference ... there can be no consensus."[5]

As Vice Chair of the U.S. Technical Advisory Group (TAG) to the ISO 14000 international committee, I see TAG members from government, industry, standards organizations, trade groups, environmental groups, and others engage on a regular basis to wrestle with passionate and divergent points of view. The TAG process is one of consensus based on ISO rules and upheld here in the United States by the American National Standards Institute (ANSI). It works most of the time (in my opinion) but it's not perfect, and there are times when one is reminded of the Tower of Babel in the biblical story. At that point, it doesn't matter what is said. The problem is too many languages are being spoken! How do we know what we know has collapsed into — what the heck are you saying?

Erik Meyers of the Environmental Law Institute (ELI) in Washington, D.C., wrote an exceptionally fine article on ISO 14001 in the March/April 1999 edition of the *Environmental Forum*, a publication of ELI. Meyers is also an active member of the TAG and of the National Accreditation Program run by ANSI and the Registrar Accreditation Board.

In the article, Meyers acknowledges the difficulties involved when competing or conflicting interests are raging in a forum such as the TAG. He likens successful resolution to the actions of the cartoon pig in the movie "Babe" and notes that: "Babe teaches the value of truly listening to what those whom you would lead have to say, and about the power of collaboration and humility." Meyers goes on to relate this to the challenge that faces industry, government, and environmentalists in coming to terms with the ISO 14001 standard.

Our first challenge is in truly listening to one another to understand the range of values and interests. Developing and evaluating data and other forms of information on EMS and ISO 14001 without predisposition and bias comes next. Struggling to find connectedness based on origins, goals, interests, backgrounds ... you name it ... follows. What happens in the public policy world and the world of business does not have to be the same for mutual trust to occur, but the benefits of convergence can't be realized without a sense of where the one connects with the other.

Pam Parry brings to this ISO 14001 world a commitment to accurate reporting and simplicity of detail. This is especially true in detailing the insights and conversations of others. The effect is to provide the reader with the sense of real-world contact where people are not always consistent but their inconsistencies are a gate to seeing complex values and interests.

I have had the privilege of knowing Pam Parry for several years. We were brought together — connected — by the emergence of the ISO 14000 developments. What she has put together is an unembellished accounting of facts and experiences minus rigorous methodoligcal discussions that are the subject of other publications. As a former researcher, I appreciate the purity of the information Pam has assembled here, and her straightforward conclusions and suggestions. I commend the reader to the following pages.

In addition, I would like to add several other sources of information for consideration. First, a number of relevant documents are available from the Pollution Prevention Clearinghouse at the EPA. Among them is a Fact Sheet on ISO 14000 standards and information on the National Technology Transfer and Advancement Act of 1995, which requires federal agencies to use, and participate in the development of, voluntary consensus standards. The number for the Clearinghouse is (202) 260-1023. One can also find information by surfing the EPA Web site <www.epa.gov> and plunging through to information within the Office of Water, the Office of Reinvention, and the Office of Prevention, Pesticides and Toxic Substances.

Another worthwhile publication is a May 1998 Report from the Organization for Economic Cooperation and Development (OECD) in Paris. The report is titled: "What Do Standards for Environmental Management Systems Offer?" It follows from an international workshop, sponsored in part by the U.S. EPA, and gives an excellent snapshot of how OECD countries view and consider the potential of EMS, including those based on ISO 14001. The publication is available on-line at <www.oecd.org> through the section on publications. The OECD contact for the project is Mr. Carlo Pesso <carlo.PESSO@oecd.org>.

Finally, though, to embrace information and grow from it, we must yield each in turn our cherished calcifications to be forged into more productive and communicative shapes, willing as Donne was to accept change which would "break, blow, burn, and make me new."

— Mary C. McKiel, Ph.D.
EPA Standards Executive
Washington, DC
May 12, 1999

1. Thomas, L., *The Lives of a Cell*; Viking Press, Inc., New York, 1874.
2. Of course this is only a partial representation of those companies in the United States that are using the standard, because certification is not required. There's no way to know how many are actually using, in whole or in part, ISO 14001.
3. Schnare, D.W., "The Stewardship Ethic — Resolving the Environmental Dilemma," *Handbook for Environmental Risk Decision Making*, C. Richard Cothern, editor, CRC, Lewis Publishers, Boca Raton, 1996.
4. Eliot, T.S., "The Choruses" from *The Rock VI*.
5. Clark, G.A., "Highly Visible, Curiously Intangible," *Science*, March 26, 1999, Vol. 283 No. 5410, AAAS, Washington, DC, pp. 2031ff.

Acknowledgments

Several people helped me in the preparation of this manuscript and deserve special recognition.

First, I'd like to thank my friends at CEEM, Inc., who introduced me to the world of ISO 14000. They helped me learn a complicated subject matter and imparted to me a passion for environmental management. Special thanks to CEEM's former publisher Brooks Cook and my former boss Mark Baker. They encouraged me to pursue this project and helped me find a good publishing home.

Second, two other friends helped me improve the overall product. Nancy Thompson edited my first draft. And then she edited it again. She provided valuable feedback and editing suggestions that ultimately enhanced the readability of the book. Her contributions have won her my highest plaudit. Cynthia Wokas provided assistance with the artwork and designs that appear in the book. Her creativity strengthened the visual appeal of my work. To both of them, I am very grateful.

Third, dozens of ISO 14000 specialists agreed to be interviewed for the book. They provided insights and pointed me to various research sources. Most of the interviews were tape recorded [when the source granted permission], and an American University student, Meaghan Lynch, worked tirelessly to help me transcribe those tapes. She also helped me with other administrative duties, like typing permission letters to sources and proofreading. Without her excellent work, the production of this book would have been much more time-consuming for the author.

About the Author

Pam Parry, assistant professor of communication arts at Taylor University in Upland, Indiana, has been writing about ISO 14000 since 1996. Previously, she was editor of *International Environmental Systems Update*, a monthly ISO 14000 newsletter published by CEEM, Inc. While in that role, she was a member of the U.S. Technical Advisory Group to ISO Technical Committee 207. She left CEEM to start her own company, Parry Communications in Alexan-
dria, Virginia, where she continued to write about the environment. Still a frequent contributor to *IESU*, Parry is the managing editor of *Business Standards*, a four-color magazine published by BSI, Inc. She is a graduate of the University of Missouri School of Journalism and holds a master of arts in journalism and public affairs from The American University in Washington, D.C. She also has taught journalism at The American University and a course on Editing for Science and Technology at the George Washington University's Center for Career Education, both in Washington. She also has written for *The Baltimore Sun*, *Washington Business Journal*, and "The McLaughlin Group" TV show.

Preface

I admit that when I first entered the ISO 14000 arena I needed an attitude adjustment. I had left the world of constitutional law and public policy for an unknown universe. Some of my business-minded acquaintances had an unusual response to the news of my transition. When I told them I was joining CEEM, Inc., to cover the environment, they got incredulous looks on their faces and said, "The environment." Granted, one reason they responded that way was they mistakenly thought I was a bleeding-heart who was too zealous when it came to things like the First Amendment guarantees of religious liberty and press freedom. They saw this new move as further slippage into the liberal milieu; after all, only fanatics cared about the environment, right? And they said the word "environment" with such a distasteful emphasis that I quickly caught myself defending my job choice — even though I was proud of my new role. I told them in no uncertain terms that CEEM wasn't the radical, tree-hugging kind of environmental firm they might have heard about in the media. No, CEEM was a for-profit company in it for the money.

Boy, did I have a lot to learn about both ISO 14000 and CEEM.

I'm embarrassed that I felt the need to defend my decision to those who had bought into this wrong-headed notion of environmentalism. The stereotype of the wild-eyed environmentalist who cares more for the spotted owl than small schoolchildren is destructive and grossly unfair. Most of my ISO 14000 dealings have been with industry leaders and corporations, but I have spent time around many environmentalists in the U.S. Technical Advisory Group to ISO Technical Committee 207 (U.S. TAG to TC 207), the group responsible for ISO 14000. I'm sincerely grateful for the work they do, and I can't understand why societal stereotypes persist. The truth is that environmentalists care about the spotted owl and other global issues specifically because they care about small schoolchildren and the world in which they live. And just like the First Amendment, I'm not sure one can be too zealous in the defense of the Earth and the world we bequeath to the next generation. I've yet to meet even one tree-bark-eating environmentalist. The environmental nongovernmental organizations [ENGOs] that participate in the U.S. TAG have my highest admiration and respect.

And I'm particularly ashamed that my defensive response ever reflected that I thought altruism should be replaced with bottom-line thinking. One of the lessons I learned in the ISO 14000 arena is that altruism and business are not mutually exclusive. In fact, the beauty of ISO 14000 is that it enables companies to do the right thing and to make money at the same time. The international standard allows companies to minimize their environmental impact on their communities while saving big bucks toward the bottom line. That should make everyone happy.

Some companies are saving hundreds of thousands — even millions — of dollars annually as a result of proactive environmental management. They have reduced waste and saved energy through innovative programs, capturing real savings. Despite those economic results, some leaders within industry still view environmental initiatives as a cost of doing business, rather than a potential savings that translates into a bigger bottom line. They are skeptical that spending money to implement and certify an ISO 14001 environmental management system will have both a quick return on investment and long-term savings.

But they are wrong.

As of this writing, ISO 14001 certifications have surpassed the 10,000 mark worldwide. The senior management of these companies believe that what is good for business has to be good for the bottom line, and they have decided that ISO 14001 is good for business.

And that's the premise of this book. I believe that ISO 14001 not only makes good business sense, but it is one of the best tools corporations have for carrying out their environmental responsibility. So, this book is written for environmental managers, regulators, consultants, ENGOs, members of the U.S. TAG, and other stakeholders interested in documenting the business benefits of ISO 14001.

If you are an environmental manager who has yet to convince senior management of the value of ISO 14001, this book is designed to help you build a business case. If you are a regulator, this book will provide you with insight into the effectiveness of industry's implementation of the standard, as well as its potential use for regulatory reform that takes us beyond command-and-control systems. If you are a consultant, TAG member, or other stakeholder, this book will arm you with specific data about the expansion of ISO 14000.

But most of all, this book demonstrates that environmental stewardship can be synonymous with profitable business practices. To support this thesis, I talked to consultants, auditors, standards writers, environmental managers, company employees, and other specialists who provide real-life insights into the tangible business benefits of ISO 14001 implementation. They helped me go from the theoretical — the potential benefits of an EMS — to the practical — the real benefits they have experienced.

But trying to pinpoint a definitive list of business benefits was difficult. Each person I interviewed offered a varying perspective on what should be included as a business benefit of an EMS. So, I have gleaned from those interviews what I perceive to be the top benefits of ISO 14001 implementation: (1) corporate culture change, (2) cost savings, (3) waste minimization, (4) enhanced relationships with the community, regulators, and stakeholders, and (5) some other intangibles. The book explores these benefits in great detail, while also offering insights into some legal issues surrounding ISO 14001 and what the new millennium holds for potential users of this young standard.

Chapter 1

A New International Standard

The end of a command-and-control regulatory system ... insurance breaks ... easier access to financing. These were among the expectations heaped onto ISO 14000 even before the voluntary series of environmental management system (EMS) standards left the starting blocks. Although the standards in the series have been developed at a varying pace, the series cornerstone — ISO 14001 — was published September 1, 1996. It provides the framework for organizations to implement an EMS. But much like Christmas morning, the heightened anticipation for ISO 14001 created a collective letdown when the standard finally arrived. Just three years into the life of the standard, some are actually disappointed that command-and-control is alive and well. And they've seen precious little evidence of insurance and financial breaks for companies sporting an ISO 14001 EMS.

But what did they expect, Santa Claus? Wouldn't you hate to be judged so harshly while you were still a toddler?

ISO 14001 does translate into business advantage. At the time of this writing, more than 10,000 certificates to ISO 14001 have been issued worldwide. Also, organizations have reported phenomenal savings and a quick return on investment (ROI). While much of the data is anecdotal, companies report many business benefits of ISO 14001: improved employee morale, enhanced relationships with regulators, waste minimization, better community relations, and process efficiencies. They also indicate that movement is afoot on the regulatory, insurance, and banking fronts, but the progress remains understandably slow (Figure 1.1).

Figure 1.1

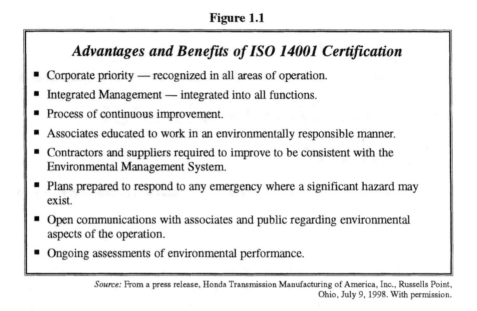

Source: From a press release, Honda Transmission Manufacturing of America, Inc., Russells Point, Ohio, July 9, 1998. With permission.

Figure 1.1

ISO 14000 Origins

The origins of ISO 14000 can be traced to the 1972 U.N. Conference on Human Environment in Stockholm, Sweden. That meeting resulted in a 1987 report that initially referenced "sustainable development," calling for industry to develop environmental management systems. Then, the United Nations convened an environmental summit in Rio De Janeiro, Brazil, in June 1992. In preparation for that meeting, the International Organization for Standardization (ISO), a worldwide organization of national standards bodies from more than 120 countries, formed the Strategic Advisory Group on the Environment (SAGE) in 1991. SAGE invested two years probing BS 7750, the precursor to ISO 14000, resulting in the establishment of ISO Technical Committee 207 (TC 207), which was tasked to develop ISO 14000. The specification document, ISO 14001, anchors the series, and it requires companies to identify their environmental aspects and impacts and then to set targets and objectives for reducing those impacts[1] (see Appendix F).

ISO 14001 is the only international EMS standard on the market, and it has been adopted as an American national standard. That fact notwithstanding, another major criticism often hurled at ISO 14001 is that certification is sluggish in the United States. At this writing, about 350 of the total certifications are in the United States, which pales next to Japan and other certification leaders.

But the certification numbers don't tell the whole story. Many companies are implementing the system but stopping short of paying for a third-party auditor to examine their EMS. These companies are certification-ready, but they are waiting to see what the market will demand. Implementation and certification are two separate business decisions. The standard allows for an alternative, known as self-declaration. Rather than having an outside third-party place its stamp of approval on the EMS, a company may choose to police itself and declare its conformance to the standard. And many companies are choosing self-declaration over certification. Another major reason U.S. companies may appear to be slow in accepting the international standard is that they have been toeing the line for a tough regulatory system for years. Environmental management systems are nothing new in the United States, where they have been prevalent for years.

A Consultant's View

Suzan L. Jackson, director of environmental services at Excel Partnership in Sandy Hook, Connecticut, discounts the notion that the certification numbers are low. "I hear that all the time," said Jackson, who provides training for companies to implement the standard. "I don't agree."

She continued, "I think people went into 14001 with much too high of an expectation. If you look at the progress of 14001 registrations and compare that to the progress of 9000 registrations at the same point in their lifetime, it is about the same. If anything, 14001 has been quicker to catch on because some people already knew about it and more people were involved in developing it."[2]

ISO 9000 is a series of standards for quality management systems that predates ISO 14000 by about a decade. ISO 9000 has its origins in BS 5750, a specification published in 1979 in the United Kingdom. ISO 9000 was published in 1987, and at this writing, more than 226,000 certifications are reported around the globe.[3]

Many credit ISO 9000 as putting the International Organization for Standardization on the map. Founded in 1947, ISO promotes the development of standardization and related activities to facilitate international trade. Headquartered in Geneva, Switzerland, ISO has churned out 11,000 international standards, but despite the volume of standards development work, ISO was relatively obscure until ISO 9000 hit the market. "We used to complain that not enough people knew what ISO was about," said ISO Secretary-General Lawrence Eicher. "Now we complain that too many people think that ISO 9000 is the only thing we do."[4]

But ISO continues to produce new standards — each business day some 15 meetings of the nearly 3000 ISO technical groups with a total of 30,000 participating experts are held around the world.[5]

And some, like Jackson, believe ISO 14001 is doing as well, if not better, than ISO 9000 did in its first few years. Registrations, another term for certifications, at least in the United States, are progressing at a reasonable level, said Jackson, who is an active member of the U.S. TAG to TC 207. She said it makes sense for companies to approach registration cautiously.

"There may not be a business driver for some companies right now," she said. "Registration is an out-of-pocket cost. Implementing an EMS that meets ISO 14001 requires an internal investment; it requires some money to be spent mainly in reallocating resources internally, because everyone thinks they don't have time to work on anything else right now. So something else has to be able to slip in order for you to be able to work on improving your EMS. But it has immediate payoff, and it is an investment rather than a cost. When it comes to registration, that is very much an individual business decision, or it should be. And some companies simply don't see any need for it yet, or any driver, and they are waiting until they see a driver.

"And I think that is a very appropriate, very reasonable response to this. In fact, that is what we advise our customers to do. Use the standard to implement or improve your EMS now, get the benefits out of it. Keep an eye on the registration drivers, and make a business decision about whether or not you need registration."

Another consultant, who served as an expert on Subcommittee 1 that wrote ISO 14001, agreed with Jackson. Marilyn R. Block, president of MRB Associates in Potomac, Maryland, said one of the reasons U.S. certifications appear to be lagging is the difference between implementation and certification; some companies are just declining to get certified.

"I'm not sure that we are lagging as far behind as the certification numbers would suggest," said Block, who was honored by the TAG in 1998 for outstanding achievement.[6]

"We've had command-and-control regs in place for a long time, and frankly that puts us way ahead of most of the rest of the world in terms of many of the kinds of activities that need to be put into place. And I think a lot of companies feel that they don't need to be certified because they are already doing many of these things."

One such company is Wilton Armetale in Mount Joy, Pennsylvania, which is the only foundry in America to self-declare conformance to the standard. David J. Schell, the company's environmental specialist, said organizations should decide why they are pursuing ISO 14001 before they jump into it. The decision to earn ISO 14001 certification is market-driven, and Wilton Armetale's market has yet to call for this particular seal of approval.[7]

"I don't think people should just go ahead and implement it because it is the newest thing out there; because in some companies, it may not be necessary," he said. "If you have a good, sound environmental management system to begin with, I don't know what real benefits you'd get from just doing ISO 14000. It is certainly a great tool to take the systems that you have and make sure it meets standards that other companies would be attaining, but some companies will implement it and some won't. We self-declared our certification about one-and-a-half years ago, and to this day, no one has forced us to get third-party audit."

Some companies aren't seeking certification, he said, because the three-year audit cycle prices are so high.

"If you are doing it because it is the right thing to do, in my mind, you don't need someone else to come in and say, 'Yeah, you're doing it, here's a certificate.' You'll know if you are doing it by seeing your waste costs come down and seeing your waste volumes decrease. That's what you need to see. A certificate on the wall isn't something people should strive for. We sell internationally in Germany, Canada, Japan, all the countries at the forefront [of the ISO 14000 movement] and not one person has asked us to get a third-party certification. So I would say right now the market is not there for our product; it might be product-specific."

Echoing Schell, Block said the cost is not prohibitive, but many companies don't yet see the value in the certificate. Implementation costs are nearly impossible to estimate, she said, noting the nature of the company and size of the business affects the cost. Also, companies that have an ISO 9000 system in place sometimes can implement ISO 14000 much cheaper, because they can piggyback procedures, building on their previous experience. Indeed, estimates from various companies have been all over the map.

"I've heard that people have done it for as low as $25,000 or $30,000 and as high as half a million," Block said. "I find both figures a little weird. One being very low and the other being incredibly high, but it really depends on where they are starting from. A company that has an existing quality system will do it for far less money than a company that doesn't."

Implementation costs also depend upon what assumptions the companies make when they come up with the numbers, she said. Block said companies use a variety of factors in determining cost. Some calculate the lost productivity of workers who are receiving training rather than producing widgets. But other companies look at the employee training cost as a nonfactor because they are already paying the salaries, so there's no out-of-pocket cost.

"You have to know what they have factored into the cost estimate in order to know what you've really got."

Cost of Certification

Another company that provides ISO 14000 training and information services also has tried to pinpoint the cost of implementing an EMS. CEEM, Inc., a member of the BSI group of companies, said the cost of certification varies according to the company size and its existing EMS. According to information on CEEM's web site, the average cost for one site within a multinational company, such as Akzo Nobel, averages about $100,000, with small- and medium-sized enterprises (SMEs) estimating an average cost of between $50,000 and $75,000 per facility.[8] Those estimates include a variety of factors depending upon the individual company. Among the cost factors is the development and implementation of the EMS, staff time, and consultant fees (see Appendix F).

Block noted that while implementation costs are hard to nail down, the actual certification costs are a bit easier to estimate. The reason? Registrars have published most of their rates. Registrars charge per auditing day and, typically, two auditors will spend two or three days evaluating the EMS, with another day to pull together a final audit report, Block said. But she quickly noted the time spent varies depending on the size and complexity of the system. Most registrars are charging, or at least listing, prices at around $1400 a day, she said. So, by calculating $1400 at eight auditor days, the total comes to $11,200. Thus, depending on the complexity of the system, it could cost between $10,000 and $15,000 to audit a single facility.

"That's not a lot of money when you consider what you'll spend to implement a system."

Block also added that some registrars are offering discounted rates at a substantial savings from the list prices, which means certification costs could be even lower.

Another highly respected consultant, Wayne Tusa, estimated the costs associated with implementation at $100,000 per site.[9] Tusa, president of Environmental Risk and Loss Control, Inc., in New York City, said that "incredibly round number" includes the cost of a consultant and doing the aspect and impact analysis that helps a facility set its objectives and targets. The actual implementation of programs to carry out those objectives and hit those targets comes with an additional cost that is very site and organization specific.

Tusa admitted that little historical data on the specific success of ISO 14001 has been collected to date, but he believed that the standard's business potential is undeniable.

"Whenever you take a step back and take a hard look at the organization and identify opportunities and liabilities in a systematic way, there are real business benefits," Tusa said. "I think that is the biggest benefit of ISO 14001. It requires you to take a comprehensive look at all your existing business activities, and in so doing, identify opportunities that have never been identified, as well as liabilities that have never been either identified or managed appropriately."

And while that's true for large firms that have compliance programs, he said, adding that it is even more true for SMEs with no systematic environmental programs in place. Ninety percent of the SMEs aren't doing anything systematically about compliance or "don't have a clue about implementing an EMS," said Tusa, who noted that is a direct consequence of a command-and-control system where there's no fiscal incentive for compliance. There's a fiscal disincentive for companies that get caught out of compliance, but scant enforcement dollars mean that most noncompliances go undetected. So, the real benefit of ISO 14001 is the rigorous look at the system.

"So the biggest tool that command-and-control has is the fear of being caught," he said, suggesting that ISO 14001 points to a better way. If companies can grasp the fact that this voluntary standard proffers clear and positive benefits, then they will be motivated to initiate programs that take them beyond compliance.

Going beyond Compliance

And going-beyond-compliance thinking is exactly what ISO 14001 is all about, according to Joseph Cascio, a consultant from Annandale, Virginia. Cascio, chair of the U.S. TAG to TC 207, has been involved with ISO 14000 from the very beginning. Cascio said an environmental manager's traditional focus has been on compliance and trying to stay in compliance while saving money. But ISO 14000 is about establishing a whole new framework and way of thinking for the corporation and, in the short term, it might not mean better compliance and cost savings, he said.[10]

"The overriding value, which I think gets discounted at this point or people don't realize, is the value of creating a different culture in the organization," said Cascio, who formerly worked at IBM. "It is bringing the employees up to a level of awareness and consciousness about how they do their jobs and the possible impacts they can have on the environment. That frankly is the biggest advantage of ISO 14000. And it is not just theoretical, because I'm getting those stories now from all kinds of people. Even organizations that have not yet fully implemented the system, they say that just trying to implement the system, just talking to the employees about what they are doing about the environment, already makes employees think differently and act differently and get different results. And they immediately begin to get savings and efficiencies even before the system is in place.

"And that is a wonderful message, because it underscores the fact that the whole purpose of this whole thing is to raise awareness. ... People just change their attitudes; they become more careful; they avoid spills; they avoid doing silly things like dumping materials down the drain or dropping them into the woods; bad habits that are easy to acquire."

Cascio said employees begin to make changes voluntarily because "there is almost a pent-up need to be responsible toward the environment. So you don't have to drag or coerce them and beat them on the head to make them do it. They do it because they want to do it, which is wonderful."

Even though companies begin to operate better and more efficiently, it is hard to prove the causality between ISO 14001 and profitability. "That's why we are always at a disadvantage in demonstrating the benefits of doing an environmental management system, because it is hard to quantify."

But Cascio — perhaps ISO 14000's biggest cheerleader — doesn't need to see bottom-line dollars to know the benefits exist. For example, he said one of his clients has a motor pool with more than 1000 vehicles. When he examined the client's environmental aspects, Cascio saw that the client was in complete compliance with regulatory requirements, such as monitoring their tanks and emissions. But by probing further, Cascio discovered a business practice that had dire environmental import even though the organization was in full compliance. Cascio asked the client if the company had trouble starting their diesel trucks in the wintertime, and the client said no. The organization didn't have trouble starting the trucks in the morning because it never shut them off. That's right, most of the trucks ran continually, all night.

"Now that's a terrible environmental story," said Cascio, who declined to name the client for confidentiality purposes. "Because they are putting pollutants into the air, wasting fuel, hurting the longevity of the vehicle, creating more problems, and yet, because there's a low environmental consciousness this was allowed to continue. With the EMS and the raising of the consciousness of the employees, we are going to change that."

That kind of anecdotal evidence is clear-cut, despite the lack of dollars that can be attached to it, he said, offering some more examples. The EMS also helped that same client optimize its vehicle routing system. Through conversations with the transportation manager, Cascio discovered he was reluctant to computerize his routes because his pay scale was tied to the number of trucks he managed. So, he had no incentive to optimize the vehicle routing, and ultimately, the fleet of vehicles' impact on the environment.

"So here is an organization that is rewarding someone to be inefficient in using the company resources," Cascio said. "The EMS will solve that. We're going to optimize vehicle routing and change the rules so the organization doesn't penalize this guy for being more efficient."

These are the kinds of discoveries and benefits an EMS will provide over and above a system that is just driven by compliance, Cascio added.

Offering another example, Cascio said one of the municipalities that the Global Environment and Technology Foundation in Annandale, Virginia, is working with has a water treatment plant. In the wintertime, the municipality would place sand on the roads when it snowed. When the snow melted, the sand ran off the road and went through the system, which meant the water had to be treated. Through the aspect and impact analysis, the plant started putting a different kind of screen in the water treatment plant that could recollect the sand. Instead of using new sand, the municipality is recycling the old sand. In addition to recycling the sand, the plant is saving on water treatment because it is processing it out before it gets to the treatment facility.

"This is not a regulatory thing. They don't have to do this. But they are finding tremendous advantage. We are finding in case after case, actually, that benefits are mainly the kinds of things that were not looked at before, because the focus was on compliance."

Cascio emphasized that this point was important because many people have complained that the standard doesn't focus enough on compliance. If the voluntary standard overemphasizes compliance, he said, companies are going to be refocusing on compliance and overlooking these new benefits.

"We're paying attention to things we never did before."

Cascio sees no disadvantage in implementing ISO 14001; the only disadvantage is not doing it, he said, likening it to weight loss.

"Maybe the disadvantage of losing weight is that you'll have to throw away all of your clothes."

Cascio, the lead U.S. delegate to ISO TC 207, summarized the four main benefits of ISO 14001. First, implementation of the standard changes the energy level of the organization through awareness. Second, raising consciousness translates into better environmental protection. Third, companies will realize actual savings through improved operational efficiencies, reduction in the use of raw materials, avoidance of liabilities, and energy. Fourth, organizations that implement ISO 14001 will be seen as responsible citizens, so their relationship will be improved with the community, regulators, and customers.

"You change the very nature of the organization," Cascio said. "I really believe that because I see it happening every day. Now that I'm working as a consultant and running around helping people do these things, I see what's happening. And it is happening. It's not just theoretical."

Notes

1. FAQs about ISO 14000, CEEM web site http://www.ceem.com, CEEM, Inc., Reston, Virginia, 1997.
2. Jackson, S. L., telephone interview, November 18, 1998.
3. Parry, P., Cooperation Is Key to Success for Telecommunication's TL 9000, *Business Standards,* North American Edition, 2(14), 1999.
4. Taylor, D., ISO's International Perspective, *Business Standards,* 4(13), 1998.
5. Ibid.
6. Block, M. R., telephone interview, October 19, 1998.
7. Schell, D. J., telephone interview, January 7, 1999.
8. FAQs about ISO 14000, CEEM web site.
9. Tusa, W., telephone interview, September 15, 1998.
10. Cascio, J., personal interview, November 6, 1998.

Chapter 2

Corporate Culture Change

Cindi Eulrich believes ISO 14001 will make a better world for her grand-children's grandchildren. Working in the machine department at Honda Transmission Manufacturing of America (HTM) in Russells Point, Ohio, Eulrich has embraced the international environmental management system (EMS): "It makes you feel better knowing that your grandkids and their grandkids are going to have a clean environment and safe world to live in."[1] And she's not alone. Lee A. Sanders, HTM environmental coordinator, said that one of the biggest benefits of ISO 14001 is the morale boost for the 550 employees that has transformed the plant — the first Honda site in North America to earn an ISO 14001 certificate.[2]

In fact, many ISO 14000 specialists agree that corporate culture change is the number-one benefit of implementing the standard. If everyone from senior management to the machinists on the shop floor is behind the effort, then environmental management becomes a corporate priority as well as a corporate reality.

"I'm basically preaching that with ISO 14000 you are going to change the culture of your organization; you are going to get people excited about this stuff, and you are going to transform your work force and get all kinds of benefits," said Joseph Cascio, a prominent U.S. consultant. "I believe people get energized when you get them to do something like this. ... When we are enthusiastic about things, productivity just skyrockets and when we are lackadaisical, then productivity goes down the drain. It is hard to come to work in the morning when you are not enthusiastic."[3]

Cascio and other consultants who help companies implement an EMS acknowledge that changing a corporation's culture requires commitment and hard work that must flow from the top. Securing senior management buy-in is the essential key to corporate culture change. But often, environmental managers meet with senior management resistance because implementing a wholesale culture change requires a significant investment of resources and time. For too long, senior managers have viewed environmental responsibility through the filter of business cost. In fact, a company will only change the way it conducts day-to-day business if management decides to do it, support it, and communicate that decision effectively throughout the organization so individuals understand how their job requirements have changed, said Wayne Tusa.[4]

"One of the great frustrations of many of the environmental departments out there, of course, is that they understand the benefits of implementing a proactive EMS, but management doesn't, or only pays lip service to that," said Tusa, president of Environmental Risk and Loss Control, Inc., in New York City.

Internal Struggle

The common tension between environmental departments and senior management is a frequent subject at ISO 14000 seminars and conferences. Among the first questions asked at virtually every ISO 14001 implementation workshop is: "How do I get senior management buy-in?" Then, participants usually follow up: "Are there some practical steps that I can take to secure management support?"

And the response often proffers several approaches.

Marilyn R. Block, president of MRB Associates in Potomac, Maryland, and an expert to Subcommittee 1 of ISO Technical Committee 207, said, "Senior management has to be convinced they want to do it. And if senior management is resistant to it, it doesn't matter what happens at the lower levels of the organization, they are never going to have the support and the resources to implement the system properly.[5]

"I think this decision is like any other business decision that management makes," she continued. "They have to consider what it's going to cost and what they are going to get back if they invest the money. I think part of the problem environmental departments or consultants have is they tend not to think about environmental issues in the same way they think about any other business issue. And it has to be handled like any other business issue."

Anton G. Camarota, president of AESIR International in Annapolis, Maryland, said that environmental issues are not always treated like regular business decisions because management doesn't know how to integrate them into the system. "Top management doesn't understand the issues around environmental management enough to integrate them into the business decisions," Camarota said. "So that's the role of the new environmental professional: to show top management how to make strategic environmental management decisions. An EMS is a tool to do that."[6]

One major hurdle to securing top management support is overcoming the fear that an outsider will expose the company to risk, Camarota said. If an auditor discovers a noncompliance, does that auditor have an obligation to report the company? Another fear is simply that an outside party will become privy to confidential information. Many of his clients are self-declaring conformance to ISO 14001 because they think the risks of certification are greater than the benefits. Those companies don't want a third-party auditor poking his or her nose into their compliance status, he said, adding that the entire EMS process is under the protection of the environmental attorney and so the progress is slow.

Business Case Argument

The way to move senior management forward is by building a strong business case, he said. Camarota said he tells his clients that an EMS is "really the only way, in the long run, to make sense of environmental management and make it a cost savings instead of a cost center. It can actually be a profit generator. That's the basic business case that I use. I tell them to look on it as a capital investment. It will have a certain rate of return, and what that [return] is depends on how they build it and the size of the facility. But it's a capital investment; it takes resources. Just like any other piece of equipment, you use it to save money and generate positive cash flow. In this case, it's mostly cost avoidance, but there are some cost reductions associated with process analysis."

Camarota continued, "I think the core business case is that you bring environmental management into the regular business management of the organization and set the stage for long-term cost reduction. That's really what the basic business case is all about. It's a technology just like any other technology, just it's a management technology."

Environmental managers must help top management understand the EMS, so the first step is basic education and training, Camarota said. The second step is reporting to management on a regular basis, giving them data they can digest. Top management needs more than just compliance reports indicating fixed costs or compliance status, he said. "You've got to give them information about the environmental performance of the firm that relates to the business objectives. And if it doesn't, then they won't buy into it."

Camarota said that the basics of culture change involve several steps. First, the company must envision and define what it wants the culture to become. Second, the company has to develop a blueprint for implementing the vision. Third, the organization must install the changes to the system and provide training for employees to fulfill the new requirements. And last, companies need to anchor the change in culture — this is the step that topples most companies, he said.

"Management has to reinforce the new values and cultural beliefs and continually reinforce the importance of the EMS," Camarota said. "And that's where the failure occurs, not in visioning, not in planning, not in installing, but in anchoring — management going out there and saying, 'This is the way things are, this is what we want it to be, this is the way it's going to work.' If they don't do that, the consequence of change fails."

Sounding like an evangelical preacher, Camarota continued, "Management has to walk the talk and make a real clear case for why they are doing it. The case has to relate to the business purpose of the organization. If employees don't understand why it's important, they won't do it. And management has to be honest about it, too. They can't be two-faced. They have to walk the talk. If they don't walk the talk, employees will just say, 'forget it.' They won't do it. Employees have to understand why the EMS is a priority in terms of the mission and vision and values of the business."

Amy E. Schaffer, senior director of environmental program coordination at the American Forest & Paper Association (AF&PA) in Washington, D.C., named two primary reasons why companies pursue EMS implementation: to respond to market pressures and to have a reasonable management approach to environmental issues.[7] For example, she said an EMS has helped one of the AF&PA members with a management problem. The company realized that several of its senior environmental staff are going to retire over the next few years, and many of the procedures, policies, and information vital to running the operation was in the heads of those individuals rather than written down in a policy manual. So, that company saw an EMS as a cohesive approach to getting this information on paper and creating a better situation for the company.

Schaffer, chair of SubTAG 4 on environmental performance evaluation, noted, "I think the bottom line is they have to be able to demonstrate that this is not an environmental add-on. This is a business decision. This has the potential of really providing some tangible business benefits, not just looking good from an environmental perspective. I think that's the key difference. And that's what I think will sell the program to the people, to skeptics."

And according to Suzan L. Jackson, the senior management of many companies is replete with skeptics. "It's very common for management to be resistant to the ISO 14001 concept," she said, adding that one of her clients is struggling with this issue.[8] "It is very, very common."

Jackson, director of environmental services at Excel Partnership in Sandy Hook, Connecticut, said environmental managers can take several approaches in trying to convince top management. One approach, she suggested, is to look for models from other companies. If other companies have reaped bottom-line results, then that success is translatable to other companies.

"You have to put it in economic terms when you are talking to management," Jackson said. "You can look at examples from other companies, but the problem is that companies just don't see themselves in a realistic way. ... We guide our customers in looking at their own business. And the environmental people — the business managers actually — need to take a look around before they dive into this at what potential opportunities they have in their own companies for business benefits and economic gain."

She said they need to "take a look at what is possible from other companies and then look inside your own company and try to find some very real examples for management of what could result."

But Jackson warned that simply finding solid examples would not be enough in most cases. Often, management will respond that the company could implement those changes without implementing ISO 14001, she said. Although companies could implement improvement projects without ISO 14001, Jackson said the truth is they will not be inclined to do so without a driver. Most companies have too much going on every day to initiate these improvements without a driver like ISO 14001.

Along those same lines, she said, is employee involvement. Traditionally in the United States, companies rely on either a single person or a small department to handle anything that might arise related to the environment. Management and most employees have no environmental responsibility in a typical company, she said.

"What ISO 14001 forces a company to do is to spread that responsibility so that every person in the company understands what his or her own personal impacts on the environment are from their own jobs," Jackson said. "And by doing that, it makes the whole system work much more efficiently, and it also makes the environmental professional's job a bit easier so maybe they can concentrate more attention on improvement projects. Right now, most environmental professionals in the U.S. don't have time to look at environmental improvement, at business improvement, because just complying with the regulations and keeping up with all of that is a full-time job. Once you have everyone in the organization understanding what their own individual roles and responsibilities are, then the environmental manager moves into more of a coordination role, and he or she can look at some of these projects that could lead to business benefits."

The standard's requirements related to training and awareness, as well as objectives and targets, force companies to get the entire work force involved, she said, adding that is a "real big benefit to a lot of companies."

When Dollars Alone Don't Make Sense

Although the usual advice for securing top management support is to make a business case, it is sometimes difficult to make a purely fiscal case, said Tusa, who has 25 years of experience in environmental consulting. Tusa tells his clients to introduce senior management to new information about the indirect benefits of an EMS and the societal need for improving environmental behavior in addition to making the usual business case. In-house environmental staff need to expose senior management to the environmental concepts and philosophies that other proactive organizations embrace. "In other words, sometimes you can't win just on the numbers, in part, because it is so hard to make the numbers case, especially since ISO 14001 has such a short track record."

But Tusa said an emerging body of evidence suggests that having a proactive environmental program has many indirect benefits, some of which are not necessarily fiscal advantages. "What I'm talking about is a positive corporate image, which has difficult-to-measure but positive impacts on how the business actually performs, its ability to capture market share, its ability to sell products, or its ability simply to negotiate its way through the business world."

In the past few years, Tusa has seen a change in attitude in the business community about the relevant benefits of being environmentally proactive. Larger companies are starting to understand that the market, the public, institutional investors, local communities, and many other stakeholders place a value on positive environmental performance, and ISO 14001 is a tool to achieve that result.

"In addition, there's a few business managers out there who, as a matter of course, believe that their organization ought to do things in an environmentally proactive way for ethical reasons," Tusa said. "There's a few companies, and the number is increasing, who have individual managers who believe that environmental issues are ethical issues, as opposed to business case issues. And there is a growing cadre of business managers who are beginning to understand that a significant portion of the marketplace feels the same way. And as they begin to understand that, they begin to change the way they make decisions for ethical reasons.

"If the environmental staff can influence or educate business managers on how others in the environmental community perceive those issues, they can change their individual perspectives and impact decision-making. That ultimately can affect how the business operates with respect to managing environmental issues."

Tusa also said that another important issue is how organizations assess environmental aspects and impacts. Today, most organizations are looking at end-of-pipe impacts, because these already are being managed for compliance purposes, he said. But implementing an EMS like ISO 14001 should result in the organization changing its mindset.

For example, Tusa said he worked with a yogurt company that was diligently trying to minimize its environmental impacts. Based on the old school of thought, the company's primary impacts were thought to be what went into the wastewater. So, to reduce impacts, the company initiated procedures to minimize process waste and spills — thus improving the quality of the wastewater. While that was an admirable goal, the biggest environmental impacts of a yogurt company could be thought of as "all those things that the cows do" and what happens to all those yogurt containers, he said. Unfortunately, the old school never even considers those kinds of impacts, he added.

"A crucial step in implementing [ISO 14001] is taking a very open-minded, hard look at all the impacts and aspects associated with all of the organization's activities and deciding which of those are significant and which of those that the EMS is to manage," Tusa said. "And almost no one has done that. Certainly no one prior to ISO 14001 has truly done that. And my gut reaction is that is because it is hard to do and requires such a change in mindset that, right now, even most of those organizations which have gone out and gotten 14001 certified have by and large only looked at end-of-pipe kind of issues."

Tusa said many companies also fail to consider the impact of their off-site activities, not because they can't identify them, but because they wrongly believe they cannot have any control over those impacts. But a good EMS can help a company manage those activities. Pointing again to the yogurt company, Tusa said the organization began putting money aside to educate farmers about the impact of their livestock, and has also modified the design of their containers to make the material more recyclable.

The key to successful implementation of ISO 14001, Tusa said, is getting the right team with the right attitude and expertise together, getting senior management on board, and then doing a rigorous aspect and impact analysis, which drives the rest of the process and results in benefits above and beyond just those associated with end-of-pipe thinking.

Beyond Engineering and Accounting

Another weapon environmental managers can employ is the use of a consultant, said Cascio, chair of the U.S. Technical Advisory Group to TC 207. "You gotta hire Joe Cascio," he said, laughing. "If you are an environmental manager, your traditional focus has been on compliance, and the only way you can justify anything is to prove you are going to do better compliance at less cost. If you are in that frame of mind and working from that paradigm, you are going to have a tough time justifying 14000. Because 14000 is not necessarily going to be cheaper and not necessarily going to mean better compliance — at least in the short term. If that is all you are trying to justify, you are not going to be able to do it. You have got to come up with a whole new approach about why it is important to do environmental management in an organization."

Cascio continued, "We're talking about a whole new concept here. It is an industrial management concept; it's industrial engineering; it's business management. That's what it is. It's a behavior approach to environmental management. It's changing the culture of your organization and the spirit of your organization, and that takes something other than a bachelor's degree in chemical engineering. I'm not saying the chemical engineer isn't smart enough; it's just that he's got to expose himself to these new ideas and these new concepts."

Cascio echoed the other consultants, saying decisions about the environment are just like any business decision. But he cautioned against looking at those decisions from strictly an accounting point of view, because quantifying benefits can be an elusive process. If a company only looks at the business case, sometimes it's not strong enough from a bottom-line point of view.

"It is a business decision of the business leader who understands these intangible kinds of things about the quality of the organization, about the quality of the work force. It takes a little bit of leadership that goes beyond accounting and engineering. It takes somebody with a little bit of vision on how changing the organization really is an improvement and worthwhile. But in order to get to that level, you have got to get to the executive. You have to get to the guy who runs the company, because he's usually the kind of guy who has that kind of vision. The accountant doesn't have that kind of vision. He wants to know the bottom line. He wants to know the dollars. Often, you can't justify the dollars.

"This is not a dollar-and-cents question you can just put on paper," Cascio continued. "It really goes beyond that. That's the problem. You have to sell this concept at a very high level. You can't sell it at the middle management level. They want numbers, engineering advantage. If you talk to the president of the company and you tell him how this is going to improve the very fiber of the organization and the people, and the enthusiasm, then you are dealing with a leader. You are dealing with somebody at that level, and they can believe you" (Figure 2.1).

Figure 2.1

---

10 Steps to Corporate Culture Change

The Environmental Staff must:

1. Educate itself on the complexities of ISO 14001.

2. Look outside to other companies for successful implementation models.

3. Look within the company for potential cost savings and process efficiencies.

4. Translate the identified benefits into financial language for senior management.

5. Educate and train senior management about the complexities of ISO 14001.

6. Envision and define a new culture for the company.

7. Develop a blueprint for implementing the vision.

8. Install the changes to the system, providing employee training.

9. Anchor the change in culture.

10. Continuously improve the system.

Source: Multiple telephone interviews with a variety of sources.

Figure 2.1

Industry Models

And that's exactly what Jack Bailey did at Acushnet Rubber Company in New Bedford, Massachusetts — he went to the top.[9]

Bailey, director of safety, health, and environmental affairs at Acushnet, said one of the selling points came from his interest in the stock market. Bailey, who trades in stocks, was monitoring the stock of SGS-Thomson Microelectronics (now named STMicroelectronics) in Rancho Bernardo, California — the first U.S. company to certify to the Draft International Standard (DIS). And in one day, SGS-Thomson stock jumped four points. Bailey emphasized that he knows no direct correlation has been proven between ISO 14000 and stock market performance, but he sincerely believed that only the best companies would be leaders in this arena, and that's what he told his boss. He told the head of the company that "only the best companies are going to have this and have it first. And I think if we want to play in that league, if we want people to recognize that we are a world-class, quality company, we better get to it, and we better not wait until the end because nobody is going to notice us. That was the basis (for the decision)."

From that point, Bailey's boss instructed him to put a plan together. Because Acushnet had a good management system in place, the company was ready for its certification audit within five months.

"It has been a door opener for us," Bailey said. "We've gotten international recognition. Some of our international customers, we beat them to 14000, and they are kind of pleased that we are certified."

Founded in 1910, Acushnet was the first company in the world known to have earned certification to ISO 9001, QS-9000, and ISO 14001. But Bailey admitted that one driver for Acushnet to become an ISO 14000 leader was the company's late entry into the quality management system standards. Acushnet Rubber Company wasn't on the cutting edge of ISO 9000 and the automotive standard QS-9000 because it took the same posture that many companies are taking toward ISO 14000. Because it looked like a lot of work and an extra expense, Acushnet decided to wait to pursue ISO 9000 when the market required them to do so.

Then the inevitable happened. Acushnet's customers wanted its supply chain to be ISO-certified, so Acushnet earned its ISO 9001 certificate on May 3, 1995, and then its QS-9000 certificate on July 31, 1996. Bailey said the company realized that there was going to be a progression, and it didn't want to get caught napping when ISO 14001 hit the streets.

"It was our philosophy that we don't want to be chasing these programs and be the last one in," Bailey said. "We decided that we should get out in front and see if these things were doable, to see if we can get them to work for us."

Bailey said a combination of the company's compliance programs and this new-found philosophy helped Acushnet down the ISO path, which has proven beneficial. "We have uncovered things that we would never have conceived would have been problems," he added. "And in some cases, we got them fixed before they created an issue for us."

But what about Bailey's model — STMicroelectronics? How did that company secure senior management support?

According to Joe Hess, the push for ISO 14001 came from the very top when the head of the company handed down a set of ten environmental commandments called the "Environmental Decalogue" (Figure 2.2).[10] The decalogue outlines the STMicroelectronics vision for environmental responsibility and sustainable development, including a goal for all of its sites to be validated to the European Eco-Management and Audit Scheme (EMAS) by 1997. The company succeeded in that goal, said Hess, health, safety, security, and environmental team leader for the Rancho Bernardo site.

The Rancho Bernardo plant earned its EMAS validation in November 1995 and its ISO 14001 certificate in February 1996. "I think generally people are proud to be associated with a company that does have an environmental ethic," he noted.

A DOE Facility

AlliedSignal Federal Manufacturing & Technologies in Kansas City, Missouri, was the first ISO 14001-certified facility within the Department of Energy (DOE) complex, according to David Huyett, technical project specialist.[11] As a DOE contractor, AlliedSignal was being asked to do more with less, so it looked for a better way to operate the three-million-square-foot plant, which manufactures nonnuclear, electronic, mechanical, and plastic components for weapons systems. The plant wanted to move from a DOE command-and-control type of environment to one that was more in line with industry standards.

"So we put forth a proposal in an effort to transition DOE orders to industry standards, and we were able to sell that concept to the DOE through a pilot study to show them some cost effectiveness in making that transition, as well as the ability to maintain a high level of performance," Huyett said, noting the 1995 pilot was global with respect to quality, environment, safety, and health.

Figure 2.2

STMicroelectronics'
ENVIRONMENTAL DECALOGUE

THE 10 ENVIRONMENTAL COMMANDMENTS OF ST

Our vision for environmental responsibility and sustainable development

In ST we believe firmly that it is mandatory for a TQM driven corporation to be at the forefront of ecological commitment, not only for ethical and social reasons, but also for financial return, and the ability to attract the most responsible and performant people. Our "ecological vision" is to become a corporation that closely approaches environmental neutrality. To that end we will meet all local ecological/environmental requirements of those communities in which we operate, but in addition will strive to:

1. **REGULATIONS**

    1.1 Meet the most stringent environmental regulations of any country in which we operate, at all of our locations worldwide.

    1.2 Comply with all ecological improvement targets at least one year ahead of official deadlines at all of our locations, worldwide.

2. **CONSERVATION**

    2.1 Energy - Reduce total energy consumed (by our manufacturing, buildings, etc.) per million dollars sold by at least 5% per year, with 25% reduction by end 1999.

    2.2 Water - Reduce water draw-down (per million dollars sold) from local sources (conduits, streams, aquifers) by > 10% per year, through conservation.

    2.3 Trees - Reduce total paper and paper products consumption by 10% per year.

3. **RECYCLING**

    3.1 Energy - Utilize alternative energy sources (renewable/co-generation) to a meaningful degree. (At least 3 pilot plants by end 1999).

    3.2 Water - For all manufacturing operations, reach a level of 50% recycled water by end 1997 and 90% by end 1999.

    3.3 Trees - Reach a usage level of 90% recycled paper, where we must use paper, by end 1995, and maintain that level.

    3.4 Chemicals - Recycle the most used chemicals - e.g., for sulfuric acid recycle > 30% by end 1997 and 80% by end 1999.

Figure 2.2

4. POLLUTION

4.1 Air Emissions - Phase out all CLASS I ODS by end 1996. Contribute where we can to reduction of greenhouse and acid rain generating gases.

4.2 Water Emissions - Meet the standards of the most restrictive community in which we operate, at all sites, for wastewater discharge.

4.3 Landfill - Achieve 100% treatment of waste at level 1 to level 4, of "Ladder Concept"* preferability, with a 1/2 life improvement goal of < 1 year.

4.4 Noise - Meet a "noise to neighbors" at any point on our property perimeter < 60 dB(A) for all sites, from end 1995.

5. CONTAMINATION

Handle, store and dispose of all potential contaminants and hazardous substances at all sites, in a manner to meet or exceed the strictest environmental safety standards of any community in which we operate.

6. WASTE

6.1 Manufacturing - Recycle 80% of manufacturing byproduct waste (metal, plastics, quartz, glassware, etc.), with a half-life for reduction goal of < 1 year.

6.2 Packing - Move to > 80% (by weight) recyclable, reused, or biodegradable packing materials (cartons, tubes, reels, bags, trays, padding) with a half-life improvement goal of < 1 year.

7. PRODUCTS AND TECHNOLOGIES

Accelerate our efforts to design products for decreased energy consumption, and for enablement of more energy efficient applications, to reduce energy consumed during operation by a factor of > 10 by the year 2000.

8. PROACTIVITY

8.1 Proactively support local initiatives such as "Clean-up the World," "Adopt a Highway," etc. at each site in which we operate, and encourage our employees to participate. Undertake to lead in establishing such initiatives, with local authorities, where none exist.

8.2 Sponsor an annual "environmental day" at each site in which we operate, involving the local community.

8.3 Encourage our people to lead/participate in environmental committees, symposia, "watch-dog" groups, etc.

8.4 Include an "Environmental Awareness" training course in the ST University curriculum and offer it to suppliers and customers.

Figure 2.2 (continued)

---

9. MEASUREMENT

9.1 Develop measurements for and means of measuring progress/achievement on points 1 through 7 above during 1995, using 1994 as the baseline where applicable, and publish results in the "environmental report" annually.

9.2 Develop detailed means and goals to realize these policies, and include them in Policy Deployment by the end of 1995.

9.3 Continue the existing Environmental Audit and Improvement program at all sites.

10. VALIDATION

Validate to EMAS standard, or equivalent, 50% of sites by end 1996, and 100% by end 1997. (In the event the validating authority is not available, this schedule can be delayed, but only for this reason.)

---

*Synthesis of European Union Strategy for Waste Management Known as "LADDER CONCEPT"

LEVEL OF PREFERABILITY	END OF LIFE TREATMENT	ECONOMIC IMPACT
1	PREVENTION - avoid waste	++ Saving at source
2	REUSE - use again for original purpose	+ Replacement reduction
3	RECYCLE - recover for alternative use	+ Material recovery
3A	RECYCLE - organic conversion (aerobic or anaerobic)	- Possible compost or methane
4	COMBUSTION WITH RECOVERY OF ENERGY	+ Energy recovery
5	INCINERATION - no recovery of energy	- Consumes energy
6	LANDFILL	- - Land consumption and contamination

Source: From STMicroelectronics' Web site. With permission.

Figure 2.2 (continued)

Once DOE signed off, AlliedSignal selected ISO 9001, ISO 14001, and the DOE's version of the OSHA Voluntary Protection Program (VPP) as the three overarching industry standards that would help the plant run more smoothly. Because ISO 14001 was only at the DIS stage at the time of this decision, AlliedSignal pursued ISO 9001 first, earning a certificate in 1995. Then, the facility implemented the VPP Star program in 1996, and the circle was complete when AlliedSignal earned its ISO 14001 stripes in May 1997.

When the ISO 14001 initiative began, Huyett was concerned that he could meet resistance from employees who were tired of the latest new movement, and management who didn't want to spend more money. So, he looked for every opportunity to integrate the three systems to ensure employee morale and management support. For example, Huyett said AlliedSignal used the same registrar for ISO 9001 and ISO 14001 so that it could maximize the opportunities for joint surveillance audits, which are conducted periodically after a company receives a certificate to ensure continued conformance to the standard.

"So everywhere we could find an opportunity to integrate the two standards, we went after those opportunities," he said. "Using the same processes, using the same registrar, using the same people in-house to coordinate the implementation and administration of those programs — all the way down the line to the point of now conducting concurrent surveillance audits for both."

Huyett, who is a popular speaker at ISO 14000 workshops, said that securing management buy-in is one of the top two or three common concerns of conference participants. "If you ever want to change the culture or the way the organization does business, you will not be successful unless you have top commitment and buy-in," Huyett said.

Acknowledging he had that commitment from the outset, he likened securing management support to the work of an auto mechanic. First, an environmental manager must recognize that ISO 14000 is a tool, a means to an end. An auto mechanic is not going to select a tool from his toolbox and say, "This looks like a neat tool. Let me see if I can figure out how to improve the performance of my car with this tool," he said. "That is not the way he does business." The mechanic will begin by identifying the needs, issues, problems, opportunities for improving the performance of the car or for fixing what is broken, then he will find the right tool for the job. Huyett said that analogy applies to any business in terms of whether it should implement ISO 14001.

"You have to start out with what are the needs, the objectives, the goals, the strategies, the tactics that that organization is currently under-taking to improve the business as a whole," he said. "And in that regard, we started out. This came down from a senior management strategic planning initiative relative to transition to industry standards, and they saw that as a strategic issue for the organization and that's what drove it for us. I was lucky to have that commitment, that buy-in from the outset. They were championing the effort and so for us it wasn't a big issue."

So what advice does he offer those environmental managers who aren't so lucky?

They have to be able to show top management how ISO 14001 meets the strategic objectives of the organization. If the environmental manager cannot tie ISO 14001 into the strategic mission of the business, then senior management won't buy in and the program is destined to fail. "You might be able to pull it off and convince an auditor that you have a good system in place, but it is not going to be effective if you don't get their buy-in. And if it doesn't meet the needs of the organization, then don't do it."

He added, "I think ISO 14000 is an effective tool for any organization that is serious about improving its environmental performance."

But he acknowledged that for some organizations improving their environmental performance may not be a business priority at this time. Perhaps they have other needs, such as cutting costs to avoid going out of business. But at some point, any organization that is going to sustain itself successfully will have to address environmental performance — it is a cost of doing business just like product quality and inspection.

One of the reasons some environmental managers have trouble getting management support, he said, is that environmental management isn't viewed as being part of the core mission of an organization. Businesses exist to make money for their shareholders and address stakeholder needs, not to protect the environment.

"Typically, environmental management doesn't contribute to that bottom line; it takes away from it. It is seen as a necessary evil, a cost of doing business. We have to do it; we'll throw the money at it and get it done. But people are starting to realize that it is bigger than that. It is an opportunity to reduce the cost of doing business and improve the performance of that business."

And that's how you grab management's attention. Once a company has support, employee involvement is easier to secure, he said. "Senior management buys in, and they drive it down. They are going to be held accountable for performance, accomplishing their objectives and targets. They are going to pass that down, and accountability is going to be passed along. So, there's going to be a handful of organizations that are held accountable, so they are going to have expectations passed down."

AlliedSignal has 3000 plant personnel in addition to a host of DOE employees, he said, noting they worked hard to raise everyone's awareness as the standard requires. One of the requirements of ISO 14001 is that employees are aware of the organization's environmental policy. During a certification or a surveillance audit, auditors are free to ask any employee about the company's ISO 14000 program and environmental policy. So, companies often spend time training employees about the standard, but translating a complex standard into everyday terms can be a challenge during those training sessions.

Huyett said the plant has a good safety culture because it is easier for employees to relate to a safety impact. Sometimes employees have a harder time grasping an environmental impact that may be two or three steps removed from their actual job. Huyett said most employees can relate to an immediate safety impact, such as a cut on their hand, more readily than an environmental impact, such as waste disposal.

So to educate employees during training sessions, Huyett tried to communicate environmental impacts in terms the employees understood. For example, he noted that every day when employees drive to work they are creating environmental impacts through the emissions of their cars and consumption of nonrenewable natural resources. Also, he pointed out that something as simple as flipping the light switch off as they are leaving their offices can conserve energy and save money. A coal fire power plant supplies the Kansas City plant with its electricity, and coal is a nonrenewable natural resource.

"You put it in terms they can relate to and they can understand, then you start to foster that awareness," Huyett said. "And once they get a little understanding and awareness in conjunction with the fact that they see that senior management is serious about it, then you start to build that groundswell of support."

Another factor that motivated AlliedSignal employees was the third-party certification system, he said. Through this process, an outside auditor is coming to the plant to validate, verify, and review the EMS, and in so doing, the auditor can interview any employee or associate on the floor relative to the organization's environmental policy. The associates know that ISO 14001 is important to management, so when someone comes in to look over their shoulders, they don't want to be the one to mess up the audit, he said.

"They don't want to be the one to be the cause of failing that audit, so then their interest piqued at that point to say, 'Hey, what is my role? What are the questions I'm going to be asked (by the auditor)? And what are the answers to those questions?' That really was the point at which you could see the light go on across the plant, and we started getting flooded with inquiries."

And earning the certificate was a tremendous morale boost, he said, particularly because the plant was the first within the DOE complex to achieve the goal. "I think some people took pride in that. There's a general concern in our culture here in the U.S. these days relative to environmental performance; people want to do their part, and in many cases they don't know how to do it or really understand what their roles are. So it gives them an opportunity now to participate and see how they can contribute."

An Environmentally Friendly Foundry

Wilton Armetale, a nonferrous foundry in Mount Joy, Pennsylvania, self-declared to ISO 14001 and became the country's first foundry to do so. David J. Schell, the company's environmental specialist, said one of the perceived benefits of ISO 14001 is that "our employees understand better how their job affects the environment, and it teaches them to look for waste in their jobs and make a conscientious effort to reduce the amount of waste that they are generating, and also look for ways to prevent waste from even being developed."[12]

Although ISO 14001 was a big accomplishment, it was not a huge morale boost for Wilton Armetale employees, he said, adding that the geographic region has an impact on that. The foundry is located in Lancaster County — what is often referred to as Amish Country — where environmental consciousness is high, so environmental responsibility is more routine than in some other areas of the country. The real impact has been "an awareness of how individual jobs really matter," he emphasized.

Like AlliedSignal's Huyett, Schell said he didn't have to wrestle with his management to secure support for the EMS, but he has met plenty of other folks who have. Wilton Armetale has a "team-based management" devoted to continuous improvement, so the management is open to employees' ideas. In 1994, Schell went to the company's board and asked if he could implement a management system — a ground-breaking notion as ISO 14001 was not even in draft form. The owners of the company backed him from the start, and when ISO 14001 was published in 1996, Wilton Armetale was poised and ready.

But Schell has dealt with other companies that had a hard time convincing senior management that ISO 14001 is a viable program to reduce pollution and waste. At the foundry, Schell generated reports that demonstrated the costs involved in implementing ISO 14001 and the return on investment in terms of waste reduction. Schell showed management that if the company reduced 10 percent of its waste how much more profit Wilton Armetale would have, and they responded, "Let's reduce it by 30 percent," he said.

"You have to think like they think and talk numbers and profit."

In 1998, Schell wrote an environmental book that talks about an imaginary, impenetrable wall between regulatory agencies and companies. And Schell said he thinks senior management's paranoia keeps the wall high. "That is a perception you have to break down and realize that environmental management isn't something that you are forced to do," he said. "It is something you should be doing as a company; it really takes a big mindset change in some companies. Some companies will perceive it as important. There are some companies that don't want to just stay in compliance."

Coming Full Circle

Honda Transmission Manufacturing (HTM) in Ohio earned its ISO 14001 certificate June 8, 1998, following a directive from Honda's president for all of its plants and operations worldwide to increase their environmental leadership. One goal is for all Honda plants worldwide to become ISO 14001 certified by December 1999, and HTM was the first plant in North America to grab the brass ring.[13]

"We have raised the environmental standards for Honda operations in North America," said Ken Hirai, president of Honda Transmission Manufacturing. "Achievement of the ISO 14001 certificate was made possible only through the leadership and participation of HTM associates. Every associate learned the principles and requirements of effective environmental management in their jobs. As we implement this international standard in our daily work, we will achieve better environmental performance and improve our business operations."[14]

Patty Whitehead, a co-project leader with environmental coordinator Lee Sanders, said she was pleasantly surprised at the associates' reaction to the program, because a majority of them enthusiastically embraced ISO 14001. Often, employees will be disinterested in the latest program because it involves extra work, she said.

"I was happy to see that the associates were concerned," she said. "To me it is obvious that it is a concern of everyone that we use fewer resources, making the future better for our children and grandchildren. Most of our associates do believe in this program. They didn't question the integrity of the program."[15]

She continued, "We talked about how this affects them. We let the associates know what this program was about, what they could do to make improvements. We stayed very basic."

Employees soon understood that something as simple as not grabbing a handful of napkins at lunch, when one will do, has an impact on the environment, she said. Cindi Eulrich, who works on special projects in the machine department, said she was stunned when she learned how much paper and water the company uses. "Now every time I throw a piece of paper away, I think about what I'm throwing away," she said. "If I throw a can away, I make sure it goes in the recycling bin. Things like that make you really think."

And that's just what Sanders had hoped to accomplish by keeping the training sessions basic and simple. For example, she said some employees were operating under the false assumption that because the company had its own wells that the water it used was free. HTM uses electricity to pump the water out of the ground and spends money to treat and dispose of it as waste, so Sanders showed employees the charges for leaving valves open. "It made a big impression on people."

Whitehead added, "This is something that everyone can feel good about. ... From the managers' aspect of saving money to the associates who are going to feel good about it because we know we made a difference in our environment. This is one of those programs in which it is a win-win situation."

And for Cindi Eulrich, the program is something that makes a tangible difference in her job — every day.

Notes

1. Eulrich, C., Whitehead, P., and Sanders, L. A., conference call, February 5, 1999.
2. Sanders, L. A., telephone interview, September 17, 1998.
3. Cascio, J., personal interview, November 6, 1998.
4. Tusa, W., telephone interview, September 15, 1998.
5. Block, M. R., telephone interview, October 19, 1998.
6. Camarota, A. G., telephone interview, November 5, 1998.
7. Schaffer, A. E., telephone interview, November 24, 1998.
8. Jackson, S. L., telephone interview, November 18, 1998.
9. Bailey, J., telephone interview, November 5, 1998.
10. Hess, J., telephone interview, March 18, 1999.
11. Huyett, D., telephone interview, November 4, 1998.
12. Schell, D. J., telephone interview, January 7, 1999.
13. Corporate Press Release, Honda Transmission Manufacturing, July 9, 1998.
14. Ibid.
15. Eulrich, Sanders, and Whitehead, conference call, February 5, 1999.

Chapter 3

Waste Minimization

"We did it for the money." That's why Acushnet Rubber Company of New Bedford, Massachusetts, pursued ISO 14001 certification, according to Jack Bailey. Bailey, Acushnet's director of environment, health, and safety, said his company found "a real relationship between doing things to improve the environment and saving money." In fact, Acushnet saves more than $2 million annually because of its proactive environmental management system (EMS).[1]

Bailey and his counterparts at other corporations agree that it is extremely difficult to pinpoint every dollar saved as a result of implementing an EMS. After all, an ISO 14001 EMS has so many intangible benefits, such as enhanced public image and avoidance of potential fines for noncompliance, that are hard to quantify in dollars and cents. Even though an ISO 14001 EMS makes their companies better places to work, they don't always know how to record that reality on the asset side of the ledger. But one business benefit of ISO 14001 — waste minimization — is more quantifiable, and some companies have captured the cost savings associated with reducing waste.

In fact, one leading U.S. consultant names waste minimization and the cost savings associated with it as the two business benefits of ISO 14001. In response to a question about the business benefits of the EMS standard, Marilyn R. Block, president of MRB Associates in Potomac, Maryland, said, "I have identified two, and they are related. One is the minimization of whatever kind of pollutants the particular company creates as part of the process. And related to that is cost savings, because as they prevent or reduce certain kinds of pollution, they don't have to spend money to treat it, store it, haul it, dispose of it. They kind of go hand in hand."[2]

And that's what Acushnet Rubber Company discovered in its pursuit of ISO 14001. Acushnet sells elastomeric products in major global markets, including the automotive, safety, electrical, and office machinery industries. The company was among the first in the United States to achieve ISO 14001 certification, and the first known company in the world to earn certification to ISO 9001, QS-9000, and ISO 14001. [ISO 9001 is a standard in the quality management system series published in 1987, and QS-9000 is a sector-specific standard for the automotive industry that uses ISO 9000 as its baseline.]

"Our customer base wants to see us have these credentials," Bailey said, noting the quality certificates are a customer requirement. While ISO 14001 certification is not yet a customer requirement for Acushnet, Bailey suspects that it will become one when the relatively young international standard matures.

"They [customers] want us to have that because it ensures that they are not going to have business interruption problems with us," he said. "We are not going to be calling them and saying, 'Well, we couldn't get our permit to make the additional parts you need. We had a problem; we had an accident, and we can't produce your parts this week.' ... It doesn't mean that we are never going to make a mistake. It doesn't mean that we are never going to have a problem. What it means is that the likelihood is reduced because we are following accepted policies and procedures."

In fact, Bailey noted the company had an accident just after it received its ISO 14001 certificate in November 1996, but the new EMS helped Acushnet avoid a tragedy. Bailey was preparing to give a presentation about Acushnet's new ISO 14001 program to compliance officers of the U.S. Environmental Protection Agency, Region 1. His speech was slated for a Wednesday morning, and Tuesday night disaster struck.

Tuesday had been a terrible day, besieged by rain and lightning storms that caused a power outage around dusk, he said. The plant went dark. Bailey was concerned about getting the employees out of the facility without incident, but their training kicked in, and the emergency procedures worked. Everyone was safely outside and waiting for the power to return. The chief engineer was smoking under an alcove when he saw a white, milky solution pouring from the roof drain. He quickly alerted the response group, and the team discovered that hydraulic oil was spilling onto the ground and heading for the river. A vacuum breaker vent line on the plant's hydraulic system extended to the roof. When the power shut down, the hydraulic rams, with heavy molds, forced the fluid back through the system. The system's tank was big enough for the fluid, but the pipes couldn't handle the overflow and it was pushing the material onto the roof. In all, 15 gallons of oil were rushing toward the river. And the plant was crippled without electricity.

Bailey informed the National Response Center because of the potential disastrous effect this spill could have on the environment, and the Acushnet employees went to work. They turned car headlights on the scene so they could see. Using portable generators, they sucked up the oil-distilled water with vacuum cleaners. After much diligence, they reclaimed most of the oil without a single drop making it to the river. The company's near disaster had been averted.

The next day Bailey walked into the presentation room and had to tell EPA officials about the accident. But he was upbeat about it. Bailey said this story demonstrates the effectiveness of ISO 14001. Without the EMS procedures and employee training involved in ISO 14001, Bailey said he's confident that the spill would have resulted in an oil slick. Not only would the oil slick have hurt the environment, but Acushnet Rubber Company would have been facing major fines and cleanup costs, he said. This cost avoidance factor is often overlooked, he added.

"Our people looked real good in terms of responding to an emergency. We got a real sense up front that this thing [ISO 14001] is substantial, and it works."

Bailey said he's glad the employees' training paid off, because training is the greatest aggregate cost of implementing and maintaining ISO 14001. The company spends about $120,000 annually on lost productivity when employees are receiving training instead of making parts. Other expenses involved with ISO 14001 implementation, such as the fee of the registrar, pale next to the price of lost productivity. But Acushnet tries to offset the cost of ISO 14001 by integrating its environment, health, and safety training — some of which is mandated by law in addition to the requirements of the voluntary standard. The training is integral to ISO 14001, Bailey said, but Acushnet would have to do some of it anyway, so he can't separate how much of the $120,000 is directly related to ISO 14001.

But even assuming all of the $120,000 is spent annually on the EMS, the company has more than recouped its investment. For example, Acushnet implemented a project to eliminate the use of trichloroethylene (TCE) for the degreasing of metal parts. The TCE elimination project alone saves the company $100,000 annually, and the company reinvests that savings into ISO 14001, so the system is self-supporting. According to an article in *Corporate Environmental Strategy,* Acushnet sports an annual cost savings of $2,135,000.[3] In addition to the TCE program, Acushnet sees an annual savings from:

- Replacing the adhesive spray with a dipping tank and centrifuge — $25,000
- Conserving water — $1,750,000
- Substituting dibasic ether (DBE) for methylene chloride — $60,000
- Conserving electricity — $50,000
- Distilling mineral spirits from used rags — $150,000[4]

Bailey said the return on investment (ROI) varied from project to project, but in many cases, they paid for themselves within one year. Those projects represent "the low-hanging fruit" or the most obvious, quick changes. But often employees can lose motivation for continual improvement, Bailey said, noting that Acushnet provides incentives for employees who save the company money. The cost savings for an improvement is shared with the department that saves the money, so the department retains and reinvests the money. This approach bolsters employee morale and productivity.[5]

For example, the TCE elimination project yielded more than expected, saving the company money on usage of water, energy, and materials. The company also started reusing chemicals, and the chemical costs dropped. The costs of that operation came down, and it became a better place to work. The reduced costs made Acushnet more competitive, earning it new business. And that competitive advantage is the reason Acushnet got into the ISO 14001 business.

"So it now becomes a better place to work," Bailey said. "There are other efficiencies that enter into it that weren't originally thought about. And they become more productive."

He continued, "We have uncovered things that we would never have conceived would have been problems. And in some cases, we got them fixed before they created an issue for us. ... We're in business for one reason and one reason only, and that's to make money. So when we can align those goals with the environmental and quality goals, it seems to work. It's when those goals don't line up you start to have problems."

Despite being an ISO 14001 leader, Acushnet is far from alone.

Helping Business Leaders

Suzan L. Jackson, director of environmental services for Excel Partnership, Inc., in Sandy Hook, Connecticut, helps companies implement ISO 14001, and one of her favorite topics of conversation is the business benefits of an EMS. She's convinced that business success and environmental improvement are related goals. In fact, business benefits are a very strong component of Excel's training and consulting work.

"Excel's overall focus is on business improvement," she said. "So, any work we do with clients on ISO 14001 or ISO 9000, we see those standards as really a tool with the focus still being on the business overall. Registration is just a distraction more than anything."[6]

Jackson said companies often become so focused on earning the certification that they forget to make sound business decisions. For example, one person who was taking a training course became exasperated with the instructor and blurted out, "Stop telling me to do what's right for my business and tell me what the minimum is that I need to do to get registered."

"Our response is, 'Sorry, but you've come to the wrong place,' " she said. "That's not what we do. But there are a lot of companies out there that are like that. For one reason or another, they have pressure to be registered. That's what they focus on, and they lose sight of what these standards are really supposed to be for."

Jackson said the main benefit of implementing ISO 14001 is the "business process improvement," which is the mid-term result. The long-term results include improved efficiency, yields, product quality, customer satisfaction, environmental performance, and reduced costs. Excel has surveyed some of its clients and other companies in an attempt to summarize some of these economic benefits. Most of the companies surveyed had some form of EMS in place prior to implementing ISO 14001 (Figure 3.1). These are some of the bottom-line benefits of ISO 14001 implementation that they identified:

- ABB Power T&D Company in Florence, South Carolina, has saved $10,000 annually by reducing paint booth waste through the use of centrifuge cleaning equipment. The company also reduced the volume of paint fumes so that it could eliminate two underground storage tanks. That action may fend off or at least greatly reduce future risks and potential liabilities.
- Comdial Corporation in Charlottesville, Virginia, has 900 employees and manufactures business communication systems. The company expanded its recycling program to include polystyrene, paper, and corrugated boxes, as well as office paper and metals. In 1995, the company reported saving $72,867 when it switched from a 1,1,1-trichloromethane to a water-based washing system.
- Dresser Industries — Gasoline Dispenser Plant — noted three ISO 14001-related actions that translate into annual cost savings. The plant, which manufactures gasoline dispensers, saves $100,000

Figure 3.1

Bottom-Line Benefits of ISO 14001 Implementation

The following summary of economic benefits was compiled from Excel Partnership's customers and other companies that have used ISO 14001 to implement or improve an EMS. Where known, the companies' size and type of industry are noted, so you can see that these types of benefits come from a wide variety of businesses. We've limited this summary to those companies that had measured specific dollar benefits. Interestingly, most of these companies already had some sort of EMS in place prior to using ISO 14001. Improvements are possible at all levels.

> *"We are one of the pioneers in environmental management and hope that more companies recognize the importance of this activity. It is not an expensive luxury but an economic advantage. To paraphrase a well-known statement, we believe 'ecology is free.' "*

Pasquale Pistorio, President and Chief Executive Officer
Formerly SGS-Thomson Microelectronics, Now STMicroelectronics

(All of its 17 sites worldwide meet EMAS requirements; 12 of these are also ISO 14001 registered.)

COMPANY	ISO 14000-RELATED ACTION	BENEFIT
ABB Power T&D Company *Florence, SC, site*	Reduced paint booth waste through the use of centrifuge cleaning equipment	**$10,000 annual cost reduction**
	Reduced volume of paint fumes in order to eliminate two underground storage tanks	**Greatly reduced future risks and liabilities**
Acushnet Rubber *New Bedford, MA* *900 employees* Develops and manufactures elastomeric products for automotive, safety, electrical, office products, and gold industries	Cut annual fresh water use from 400 million gallons for 25 million gallons	**Annual savings of $100,000**
	Eliminated use of trichloroethylene (TCE) from 40,000 pounds in 1989	
	Reduced electricity usage by more than 1.5 million kilowatt hours	**All EMS improvements add up to a savings of $2 million annually**
Comdial Corporation *Charlottesville, VA* *900 employees* Manufactures business communication systems	Expanded recycling programs to include expanded polystyrene, all paper, and corrugated boxes, in addition to office paper and metals	
	Switched from 1,1,1 Trichloroethane washing system to water-based system	**$72,867 cost savings in 1995**

Figure 3.1

COMPANY	ISO 14000-RELATED ACTION	BENEFIT
Department of Defense *Texas Natural Resource Conservation Commission* Partnership program involving state regulators and DoD staff visiting five military bases to identify pollution prevention opportunities	Reduced hazardous waste generation by 8,000 pounds Reduced water usage by 44,000 gallons Other improvements implemented from partnership	**$21,000 annual savings**
Dresser Industries - Gasoline Dispenser Plant *1,000 employees* Manufactures gasoline dispensers	Eliminated phosphate pretreatment plant for wastewater Initiated program to blend used oils and off-specification gasoline for use in on-site boilers Converted from silk-screened labels to vinyl decals	**$100,000 annual savings (92% ROI after first year)** **$10,400 annual savings (23% ROI after first year)** **$995,000 annual savings (44% ROI after first year)** **Eliminated future risks and liabilities**
Hitachi Research Laboratory *Hitachi City, Japan* *1,300 employees* Research and development facility	Turn off lights during lunch time Improved system for ordering chemicals and supplies	**$60,000 annual savings** **Use fewer supplies now and save money**
Philips Electronics *250 facilities worldwide in 60 countries (104 facilities in U.S.)* Manufactures and distributes electronic products Set corporate goals of:	25% reduction in energy usage per facility Reduce packaging materials by 15% Incorporate concepts of ecodesign and sustainability into all products	**Achieve ROI for ISO 14001 implementation within 2 years**
Warner-Lambert *Lititz, PA, facility*	Eliminate CFCs by installing chilled water system Waste minimization Reduced waste streams by 34% Reduced packaging wastes	**$164,000 annual savings and improved operations** **$100,000 annual savings** **$1 million annual savings**
Western Digital Corporation	Installed motion-detecting lighting Eliminated disposable packaging	**Over $100,000 annual savings**

Source: Excel Partnership, Inc.'s Implementing an ISO 14001 EMS training course. With permission.

Figure 3.1 (continued)

every year by eliminating the phosphate pretreatment plant for wastewater. The ROI for this project was 92 percent after the first year. Dresser Industries also initiated a program to blend used oils and off-specification gasoline for use in onsite boilers, netting a $10,400 annual savings. But the biggest annual savings — $995,000 — came from converting silk-screened labels to vinyl decals; this improvement eliminates future risks and liabilities.

- Hitachi Research Laboratory in Hitachi City, Japan, saves $60,000 every year because its 1300 employees turn off the lights during lunch time. The research and development facility also saves money by improving its system for ordering chemicals and supplies.

- Warner-Lambert in Lititz, Pennsylvania, reported a $1 million annual savings because it has reduced waste streams by 34 percent, and it has reduced packaging waste. Other waste minimization projects save Warner-Lambert $100,000 annually, while installing a chilled water system results in another $164,000 annual savings in improved operations.

- Western Digital Corporation also saves more than $100,000 annually because it installed motion-detecting lighting and eliminated disposable packaging.[7]

Excel Partnership uses this four-page table of economic benefits in its implementation course to help show companies how to build a business case for ISO 14001. Building a business case is a necessary first step, Jackson said, adding that environmental managers will need to demonstrate bottom-line benefits to secure senior management support.

"Management is so focused on the bottom line because they won't be in business if they can't make money. So anything in the business really has to be brought into those terms. What is the bottom-line effect or the economic benefit? Many companies don't measure their improvement — particularly their economic improvement [as a result of ISO 14001 implementation]. And they say, 'Oh yeah, it has done some great things,' but they really can't quantify it.

"Well, if you start off with this approach, then you are going to be more likely to measure where you are starting from and to quantify the economic gains that you do achieve. And that is extremely important."

Altruistic Bent

Dave J. Schell, an environmental specialist with Wilton Armetale in Mount Joy, Pennsylvania, said companies should implement environmental management systems because it is the right thing to do. His motivation is purely altruistic — companies have a responsibility to reduce their environmental impact on their communities. But in the case of ISO 14001, Schell said companies can do the right thing and make a profit.

Wilton Armetale, a nonferrous foundry located in Lancaster County, manufactures tabletop and serveware pieces sold around the globe; these products are made from Armetale metal, which is a specially blended, nontoxic, aluminum-based alloy.[8] The company also has the distinction of being the first foundry in the United States to self-declare its conformance to ISO 14001.

Wilton Armetale has drastically reduced its waste cost. Within the first three years of the environmental program, the company cut its waste by 70 percent. But Schell quickly added a caveat, noting that waste reduction is due to the company's entire environmental program, which includes ISO 14001. (Most environmental managers were quick to point out these waste reductions could be accomplished without ISO 14001, but they also said the EMS standard was a good tool for implementing the waste minimization programs.) Wilton Armetale also has reduced its solid waste volume by 44 percent and its total landfill material by 24 percent. Schell said the company doesn't release what those percentages mean in terms of cost savings because it is a privately-owned corporation, but "we've reaped a lot of money out of it."[9]

The program paid for itself within the first six months of implementation, the rest goes to the bottom line, and it is annualized, he said. But Schell thinks the company is entering a maintenance phase without much room for improvement. "We found that this year we hit a plateau," he said. "I don't know how much more we are going to be able to save. Right now, unless we do something real major, we pretty much hit bottom [on how low we can go]."

The World's Second Largest Corporation

Ford Motor Company, founded in 1903 by Henry Ford, became the first and only automotive company to certify all of its plants around the world to ISO 14001 — that's a total of 140 plants in 26 countries. And they did it in three years. The company reports that ISO 14001 has led to significant improvements in energy use, waste disposal, water treatment, recycling, and air pollution. Through packaging efforts, Ford has kept 163 million pounds of waste — enough to fill 120 football fields waist high — out of landfills in just two years.[10]

"Being ISO 14001 certified means that experts outside of Ford agree that we are world-class in terms of environmental management," said Bob Transou, group vice president of manufacturing in a company press release. "Achieving ISO certification also highlights Ford's philosophy that environmental excellence is an element of both good business and corporate citizenship."[11]

Ford has more individual sites certified in the world than any other company, and the company's ISO 14001 efforts have begun to pay dividends in terms of the environment and cost savings. As part of the company press release, Ford offered some environmental success stories at a variety of its plants:

- St. Louis Assembly Plant — Located in Hazelwood, Missouri, this site instituted a waste minimization program in accordance with ISO 14001, leading to a 35 percent reduction in the amount of solid waste going to the municipal landfill. New recycling initiatives have kept about 600 tons per month of solid waste out of the landfill.
- Van Dyke Transmission Plant — In 1998, the governor of Michigan gave this Sterling Heights facility the state's Clean Corporate Citizenship Award for its ISO 14001 efforts.
- St. Thomas Assembly Plant — The Recycling Council of Ontario gave this plant the Gold Award for its waste reduction, reuse, and recycling efforts. The waste deposited in the landfill between 1992 and 1997 has been slashed by 78 percent, from 5310 metric tons to 1174 metric tons.
- Chicago Assembly Plant — This facility has reduced its solvents used for paint cleanup by 61 percent, from 448 tons a year in 1995 to 176 tons a year in 1998. The site achieved this reduction by eliminating spray solvent cleanup, purge system optimization, and replacing VOC-containing solvents with products containing no or low-volatile organic compounds. This achievement greatly benefited the environment by lowering the amount of VOCs released into the air.
- Tulsa Glass Plant — This Oklahoma plant recycled more than 3 million pounds of scrap metal and 43,000 tons of glass in 1998.
- Essex Engine Plant — This Windsor, Ontario, plant reduced the solid waste going to landfill by 350 tons a year.
- Sterling Plant — This Sterling Heights, Michigan, facility saves 170,000 gallons of water a day, reaping $59,000 annually in cost savings. It saves water by cooling its tower tanks and repairing float control devices and bypass switches.

- Windsor Engine Plant — This Ontario site saves $140,000 a year through the energy savings of 6 million kilowatt hours per year by shutting down equipment in production areas during the weekends and when the shifts are over.
- Hermosillo Assembly Plant — This Mexican facility, working with its waste management supplier, has cut by 60 percent the waste it sends to landfills by systematically segregating waste.
- Kentucky Truck Plant — This Louisville plant saves $150,000 annually on its electric bill by optimizing air compressor operation and reducing the facility's compressed air pressure from 105 PSI to 95 PSI.
- The Louisville Assembly Plant — This Kentucky facility has earmarked $100,000 in annual savings from its ISO 14001 program. As part of the plant's ISO 14001 efforts, the plant has reduced its natural gas usage, which resulted in the savings. The energy reduction was achieved by switching from steam-based air tempering coils to electrical-based, and shutting down boiler operations when they are not in use.
- Ohio Assembly Plant — ISO 14001 also helped the Avon Lake site save more than $15,000 through an improvement program in which 55-gallon drums are no longer scrapped. The drums are cleaned, melted, and reused as raw material for engine blocks. More than 2300 steel drums were recycled in 1997.
- Atlanta Assembly Plant — The Georgia facility reduced its wastewater treatment sludge from 745.5 tons in 1995 to 470.6 tons in 1996 and 329.9 tons in 1997 for a total reduction of more than 55 percent. The plant managed the reduction by changing and optimizing chemical usage (eliminating lime and ferric chloride, and using only calcium chloride) and the introduction of the emulsified paint recycling (Philip) system.

Through its Total Waste Management system, Ford gives monetary incentives to suppliers for reducing their waste. For example, Ford used to pay by the barrel or the load, but now the company pays waste removal suppliers on a scale that doesn't reward for quantity. Now, Ford might pay a set amount by the month or by the number of automobiles rolling off the assembly line.[12]

"We committed to completing the ISO process for our plants just three years ago," said Transou. "It was a very challenging stretch, but we feel it's important to be environmental leaders in the communities where we live and do business. ... Working under the ISO framework, we looked at literally every environmental aspect in every plant. At Michigan Truck, for example, there are already huge decreases in the amount of water used — almost a million gallons a day — and the amount of energy saved."[13]

Michigan Truck also instituted a program that replaced 1975 fluorescent bulbs with metal halide bulbs, saving the plant $66,000 annually in energy costs.

Christopher H. Porter, environmental management manager in Ford's Environmental Quality Office in Dearborn, Michigan, said Ford coalesced around ISO 14001 because, as a global company, it was looking for an opportunity to rally around a particular system, and ISO 14001 is the only internationally recognized standard.

"We felt that we could (reap) cost savings," said Porter, a member of the U.S. Technical Advisory Group to ISO TC 207. "We thought we could improve our compliance and the overall business."[14]

Porter said Ford registered nine facilities in 1996, 22 sites in 1997, and more than 100 in 1998 to meet its three-year deadline.[15]

Rolf W. Quisling, counsel, Office of the General Counsel in Dearborn, said Ford didn't make its decision to pursue worldwide certification to the standard based on a cost analysis. ISO 14001 has subtle benefits that are hard to measure, he said, asking how to measure the effect on employees. "We see that it has a positive effect you can't measure specifically," he said.[16]

In the United States, the business benefits are small in terms of sales, he said, adding that the main benefits will be an enhanced corporate image and improved compliance. Implementing the standard at all of its sites has improved Ford's ability to comply, he said.

"So one of the big business benefits is in terms of reducing exposure to fines."[17]

One of the criticisms of ISO 14001 is that it does not require companies to comply, he explained, but he thinks that's a false conception. Theoretically, a company could implement an EMS that doesn't comply with its country's environmental regulations and still be certified because of the flexibility of ISO 14001. Designed to fit any size organization and business sector, ISO 14001 allows the company to set its own objectives and targets, essentially letting the company say what it is going to do or accomplish, and the third-party auditor checks to see if the company does what it says it's going to do. So, technically, a company could earn a certificate without being in compliance. But Quisling said that would not happen in the practical application of the standard because of the standard's emphasis on continual improvement, including the commitment to comply with legal requirements.

"That argument is based on paranoia or a misunderstanding of the process," he said. "If you set out to try to beat the system and didn't want to comply, you might be able to do so for a short time. But you couldn't make the three-year renewal. You are going to have to continuously improve your ability to comply."[18]

He said the EMS standard enables companies to identify those areas where they might accidentally slip out of compliance, he added. In fact, Ford is so confident of ISO 14001's effectiveness that in February 1999 the company sent a letter to its suppliers encouraging them to align their EMSs with the standard.

Ford Motor Company's commitment to ISO 14001 grows from its strong commitment to the environment that was embodied by its founder who was a conservationist in his day. "Mr. Ford believed that industry and nature should coexist and together serve humanity," according to the company's 1998 environmental report. "His efforts at using agricultural products such as soybeans in the manufacture of automotive components and his interest in the study of birds were notable in his time.

"As the company grew and built factories to meet customer demand for its popular Model T, Mr. Ford also set aside land to grow crops for use in company products. In 1915, the coil cases of the Model T were partially made of wheat gluten. In the 1930s, the company replaced some steel with plastic made of soybeans as a lighter and environmentally friendly material. By 1935, two pounds (0.91 kilograms) of soybean products went into every Ford car.

"In 1908, Ford Motor Company built its first electric vehicle. As advances in fuel and emission technologies ushered in an era of cleaner vehicles, the company began to manufacture more environmentally friendly automobiles. Ford has been a leader in alternative-fuel vehicles for more than three decades."[19]

That family and corporate commitment continues today, and is reflected in the company's environmental policy which was issued in 1989 (see Appendix A). The policy shapes the way Ford does business, and ISO 14001 helps the company meet its lofty goals.

In its 1998 Environmental Report, Ford highlights the ISO 14001 program of its Lima Engine Plant in Ohio, which earned its certificate in December 1996. Within one year of having a system in place, the Lima plant had reduced its water consumption by nearly 200,000 gallons per day, and increased the use of returnable packaging from 60 percent to 99 percent on its newest engine product.

One of the first four Ford manufacturing plants in North America to earn a certificate, Lima Engine invested more than $220,000 in direct training costs, spending more than 5600 employee hours on meetings, training, internal audits, and third-party audits. Through its aspect and impact analysis, Lima Engine identified 30 significant environmental aspects, ranging from wastewater discharge and material handling to solid waste disposal. Then, the 2100 employees at the 2.4-million-square-foot facility set objectives and targets to curb these impacts. Lima Engine passed its certification audit, crediting three factors for the success of its program. First, the teamwork of the employees and commitment of the personnel. Second, Lima Engine had an ISO 9001 management system in place and that helped expedite the ISO 14001 implementation. Third, the site used the company's intranet site — the Ford Web — to disseminate information about the program, reducing the need for paperwork documentation.

"The employees of Lima Engine are proud of the Ford Environmental System and their ISO 14001 certification," according to the environmental report. "The plant has forged close ties with environmentally related organizations in the surrounding community. A Lima Engine representative serves on the North Central Ohio Solid Waste Management District Policy Committee and the Allen County Local Emergency Planning Committee. Neighbors from the community have visited the plant and have seen how the Ford Environmental System supports waste minimization, pollution prevention, and emergency response."[20]

Huge Pharmaceutical Company

Bristol-Myers Squibb (BMS), one of the largest pharmaceutical companies in the world, also has reaped tremendous waste reductions from its environmental programs. BMS was the first large, multinational corporation to self-declare to the published standard in May 1997.[21] BMS is a diversified worldwide health and personal care company whose principal businesses are pharmaceuticals, consumer products, nutritionals, and medical devices. It is a leading maker of innovative therapies for cardiovascular, metabolic, and infectious diseases, central nervous system and dermatological disorders, and cancer. The company also is a leader in consumer medicines, orthopedic devices, ostomy care, wound management, nutritional supplements, infant formulas, and hair and skin care products.

BMS developed its own environmental, health, and safety (EHS) program based on the 16-point voluntary charter called the International Chamber of Commerce Business Principles for Sustainable Development, which BMS signed in 1993.[22] In addition to the company's EHS, the company's sites across the globe are seeking ISO 14001 certification, but BMS has left the business decision of whether to pursue the standard up to the individual sites.

George Nagle, BMS corporate senior director, said, "Our company believes ISO 14001 is a very good framework for establishing an EHS management system, and we implemented a program that is consistent with that worldwide. Within our own company, when you get to the third-party aspect of that, we decided to let that be a facility-by-facility, country-by-country decision."[23]

At the time of this writing, nine BMS manufacturing and research facilities had earned certificates, with more working on it. "All [sites] have a management system in place that is aligned with 14001, but each facility decides whether to get the third-party sticker," he added. "It was more a pull than a push within our company; in certain regions of the world and for certain product lines, it is very beneficial."

"At Bristol-Myers Squibb, we work hard to prevent and minimize pollution, to reduce accidents, conserve resources, and promote EHS protection, education, and technology transfer around the globe," Thomas M. Hellman, BMS vice president, environmental affairs, occupational health and safety, wrote in the company's 1997 EHS Report.[24] The report highlights all of the environmental initiatives, including those that expand beyond BMS's ISO 14001 program. Hellman highlighted one innovative idea that cut waste. A cross-functional team at BMS's Mead Johnson Nutritionals facility discovered that a by-product generated by a supplier in the production of hydrolyzed whey for European markets was a terrific match to the nutritional requirements of a medical-nutritional product under development. The supplier was disposing of this by-product prior to this discovery, but now that the by-product has been incorporated into the new product formula, that waste has been eliminated.[25]

"Through innovative thinking, our employees are fulfilling our customers' needs while eliminating the generation of waste at our supplier's facility," Hellman added.[26]

BMS's web site — one of the best EHS sites the author has visited — provided business profiles of environmental challenges at various BMS sites throughout the world. The Pharmaceuticals Group, for example, has decreased its releases of 10 high-priority solvents by 48 percent since 1988, anticipating to reduce the emissions by 94 percent in time for the new millennium. Other EHS highlights include:

- At a plant in Agen, France, employees have instituted a program that saves more than 1600 pine trees annually as well as big bucks on the corporate bottom line. The new system recycles pallets. The facility's main supplier provides its materials on "rented" pallets that then are reused to ship finished products; the renter gathers the pallets from either wholesalers or warehouses. The supplier pays $4 per pallet — a significant savings as new pallets cost between $8 and $12 apiece. Those same employees save BMS another $600,000 every year by reusing shipping cartons; they save 1.2 million cartons annually.

- A site in Barcelona, Spain, is pursuing ISO 14001 certification. But even before they earned the certificate, employees at this facility instituted several waste minimization programs: solvent use is down by 28 percent, glass consumption has been reduced by 10 percent, paper and cardboard waste has been cut 15 percent, water usage is 23 percent lower, and electricity consumption has been reduced by 8 percent. Also, they have increased their recycling efforts by 11 percent (by weight).

- A Cali, Colombia, plant nets $15,000 annually through an energy program that reduces energy costs.

- A Confienza, Italy, facility cuts its water usage from 40,000 gallons a day to 800 gallons through the installation of a closed-loop, cooling-water recirculation system.

- When the Moscow facility earned its ISO 14001 certification in January 1998, BMS was the first company in Russia to be registered to the EMS standard.

- In Statesville, North Carolina, the plant earned the 1996 Governor's Award for Excellence in Waste Reduction. The facility no longer uses shrink wrap to pack finished product cartons, eliminating more than 4.5 million linear feet of polyolefin film and saving more than $230,000 annually. The site netted that benefit without so much as a penny of capital investment.

- A recycling program in Warsaw, Indiana, saved the plant nearly $850,000 in revenue in 1997. The program recycled more than 800,000 pounds of cardboard, paper, aluminum, steel, and other metals.

BMS expanded its ISO 14001 influence in November 1998 by becoming the first known pharmaceutical company to encourage all 15,000 of its suppliers to align their EMSs with ISO 14001. In a November 5 letter, BMS stopped short of making ISO 14001 a requirement. Rather, BMS suggested that "this would be mutually beneficial" because "BMS would be assured of receiving the highest quality products and services from suppliers and contractors, while causing the least environmental impact. Your company could benefit from potential new markets, and potentially better reception before governmental regulators" (Figure 3.2).

Nagle said this action has a significant business benefit. "Our company has established a vision or goal of having environmental, health, and

Figure 3.2

November 5, 1998

Dear Business Partner,

Bristol-Myers Squibb Company (BMS) is committed to protecting the environment and the health and safety of our employees, our customers, and the public. As part of our commitment, BMS requires our contractors and suppliers to comply with the applicable environmental, health, and safety (EHS) governmental regulations. BMS believes that it is important to share the Company's EHS commitment with you as part of its pledge to support overall civic and environmental progress.

One aspect of the BMS commitment relates to ISO 14001, which was developed by the International Organization for Standardization (ISO) in 1996 for the purpose of promoting pollution prevention and continuous improvement through sound environmental management systems. Today, there are over 5,400 ISO 14001 certified businesses worldwide. (You can obtain more information on ISO 14001 from ISO's website at www.iso.ch/9000e/9k14ke.htm.) In May 1997, BMS became the first large, multinational corporation to self-declare conformance to the finalized ISO 14001 environmental management systems standard. Since that time, BMS has certified nine facilities around the world to ISO 14001 using internationally accredited registrars. BMS plans to have more ISO 14001 certified facilities in the future.

BMS encourages you to align your environmental management systems with the requirements of ISO 14001, and to consider the benefits of certification to that standard. If you align your organization with ISO 14001 requirements, this would be mutually beneficial. BMS would be assured of receiving the highest quality products and services from suppliers and contractors, while causing the least environmental impact. Your company could benefit from potential new markets, and potentially better reception before governmental regulators.

A detailed description of our EHS management systems, programs, and performance is available on our website at www.bms.com/EHS/Environment/index.htm. BMS encourages you to join our EHS leadership efforts by adopting policies and practices consistent with such leadership.

Please contact George Nagle with any questions you may have regarding our EHS commitment and ISO 14001. He can be reached at (315) 432-2731, or e-mail at Gnagle@useemail.bms.com. BMS looks forward to working with you to make excellence in EHS a matter of competitive advantage for both of our companies.

Sincerely,

Thomas M. Hellman
Vice President, EHS
Bristol-Myers Squibb Company

Richard R. Nabb
Vice President, Global Strategic Sourcing
Bristol-Myers Squibb Company

Source: A Letter from Bristol-Myers Squibb to its Supply Chain. With permission.

Figure 3.2

safety management systems that go beyond compliance. And we certainly recognize the business benefits of that, and it just makes good business sense to then encourage that on the part of our suppliers that are truly a part of our supply chain. Number one, it just makes good social sense and environmental sense. It also makes good sense from a supply, continuity, reliability point of view. In the sense if you are dealing with suppliers that have program management systems in place that go beyond compliance, you are much, much less likely to run into supply interruption kind of issues involving EHS kind of impacts. The other thing is to the extent that they are proactive in their leadership programs, they are going to experience business benefits that hopefully then reduce their costs, which then hopefully get passed on to us in terms of what we pay for goods and services."[27]

BMS is one of at least four mammoth corporations known to encourage their supply chains to consider ISO 14001. Ford Motor Company mailed its letter in February 1999. IBM urged more than 950 suppliers to align their EMSs with ISO 14001 in an April 1998 letter. Xerox followed suit in November 1998, sending a letter to its 30,000 suppliers telling them that conformance to ISO 14001 or the European Eco-Management and Audit Scheme (EMAS) is going to become a requirement for doing business with The Document Company.[28]

Baxter Takes Big Bucks to Bank

Baxter International, Inc., headquartered in Deerfield, Illinois, has an impressive environmental record, racking up award after award, but from a bottom-line perspective, the company's environmental initiatives have translated into millions of dollars saved and millions more realized in terms of cost avoidance. Baxter saved almost $14 million in 1997 through its environmental initiatives. Baxter reaped another $86 million in cost avoidance in 1997 from environmental efforts dating back to 1990. In other words, Baxter would have spent $100 million more in 1997 for raw materials, production, processes, disposal costs, and packaging if the company had not implemented its environmental initiatives in 1990. Total environmental program costs were 0.3 percent of the company's sales in 1997.[29]

A global medical products company, in 1998 Baxter issued its 1997 Environmental Health & Safety Performance Report on the environmental program of 81 sites within Baxter, including 58 manufacturing, laboratory, and research facilities, and 23 nonmanufacturing facilities. Baxter reported that it incurred no government environmental fines in 1997, and did not have any significant chemical spills that year. The report also noted several accomplishments in the area of waste minimization:

- Baxter slashed its toxic and chlorofluorocarbon (CFC) air emissions per unit of production by more than 42 percent between 1996 and 1997, lowering them 161,000 pounds. The company has drastically reduced toxic and CFC air emissions by nearly six million pounds since 1988.
- Baxter also lowered its nonhazardous waste generation eight percent per unit from 1996 levels, beating a company goal. Since 1989, off-site nonhazardous waste disposal has been cut by 33 million pounds. "This equals a 43-percent overall reduction in the face of increasing production and a 64-percent per-unit reduction," the report notes.
- The company recycled 59 million pounds — including two million pounds of paper — in 1997.
- Baxter's total energy consumption increased from 5.7 trillion British Thermal Units (BTUs) in 1996 to 5.8 trillion BTUs in 1997, representing a one percent increase as production grew, and a four-percent per-unit reduction.
- Between 1996 and 1997, packaging decreased one percent, or one million pounds.

These terrific results and savings are the result of proactive environmental management, but not necessarily in the form of ISO 14001. Baxter has been a leader in EMSs since the early 1990s, setting a company standard and program in place in 1991. Called state-of-the-art (SOA) environmental management system standards, Baxter's program involved a third-party verification. Four years later, Baxter also initiated health and safety (H&S) management standards, which were integrated with SOA in 1997. The company calls the new EHS management system standard BEHSt — the Baxter Environmental, Health & Safety standard — which is compatible with ISO 14001.

"We hope to have all of our manufacturing sites certified to BEHSt by the year 2000, and our nonmanufacturing sites by 2002," Verie Sandborg, manager of corporate environmental, health, and safety at Baxter International, told CEEM's *International Environmental Systems Update (IESU)*. "We made the standard ISO-compatible. Anybody certified to the BEHSt standard would have everything in place to get [ISO 14001] certified — they would just have to do the administrative part of it."[30]

In fact, 24 of Baxter's facilities have earned ISO 14001 certification, and another 30 sites have committed to achieving certification as of March 1999.

"Basically, we have left [ISO 14001 certification] up to each facility as a business decision," said Peter Etienne, corporate counsel for environmental, health, and safety at Baxter, in *IESU*. "We realize that ISO has a wider acceptance. It has market advantages in certain regions, though not everywhere.

"We certainly want to position our facilities to be ISO-ready," Etienne continued. "We tried to align BEHSt pretty closely to ISO 14000, with some very minor differences that are pointed out in the standard. The incremental difference between BEHSt and ISO 14001 is almost nonexistent, it's really negligible."[31]

Whether all Baxter's sites eventually pursue ISO 14001 remains to be seen, but one thing's certain: this company shows a direct correlation between environmental management systems and the bottom line (Figure 3.3).

Energy Savings

Consultants and industry representatives agreed one major area of cost savings involves energy efficiencies. Wayne Tusa, president of Environmental Risk and Loss Control in New York City, said that ISO 14001 should result in an increased focus on pollution prevention, design for environment, and energy conservation. "Energy in the U.S. has been so cheap for so long, most companies have not focused on minimizing their energy costs," Tusa said. "And the reality is that with today's technology companies can easily reduce energy costs 25 to 50 percent with returns of two to three years. So most companies ought to implement ISO 14001 and not be worried about economic payback since you can pay for your entire ISO program through energy savings alone."[32]

For more information, Tusa pointed to the U.S. Environmental Protection Agency's Green Lights and Energy Star Programs. Many companies report saving money through energy efficiency via implementing EMSs, still others have seen results through participating in a voluntary government partnership of the U.S. Environmental Protection Agency called the ENERGY STAR® Buildings program. The program is designed to motivate companies to manage their energy usage and save money. For example, the energy to run a typical office building costs U.S. companies $1.50 per square foot, but through this program, the energy cost could be cut by 30 percent.[33]

Figure 3.3

BAXTER INTERNATIONAL
Detail on Income, Savings, and Cost Avoidance
From 1997 Activities
($ in millions)

	Savings & Income	Cost Avoidance	Total Financial Benefit
Ozone-Depleting Substances Cost Reductions	1.4	0.3	1.7
Hazardous Waste Disposal Cost Reductions	(0.1)	0.1	0
Hazardous Waste Material Cost Reductions	(0.4)	0.2	(0.2)
Nonhazardous Waste Disposal Cost Reductions	0.0	0.2	0.2
Nonhazardous Waste Material Cost Reductions	(0.1)	3.0	2.9
Recycling Income	4.1	0.5	4.6
Energy Conservation Cost Savings	(0.9)	4.2	3.3
Packaging Cost Reductions	1.3	*	1.3
Total Savings	**5.3**	**8.5**	**13.8**

*Not applicable

Source: Environmental, Health & Safety Performance Report, Baxter International, Inc., issued in 1998.
With permission.

Figure 3.3

"ENERGY STAR® Buildings has changed how we look at our business," said Thomas Stemberg, chief executive officer at Staples, Inc. "As we reduce the cost of energy, we can pass some of those savings to our shareholders in the form of higher profits, and to our customers in the form of lower prices."[34]

According to an EPA brochure, several organizations have seen incredible results:

- The City of Hope National Medical Center has an annual energy savings of 22 percent, translating into $1.7 million in annual cost savings.
- The *Atlanta Journal & Constitution* has seen an annual energy savings of 28 percent, resulting in $900,000 in savings every year.
- Honeywell, Inc. also noted a 28 percent annual energy savings, realizing $3 million in annual cost savings.

Companies across the globe are beginning to see real savings through waste minimization, and with energy consumption, millions can be earned with virtually no capital outlay. That reality ought to impress any stockholder. And ISO 14001 is one tool for finding energy savings and other waste reductions.

Notes

1. Bailey, J., telephone interview, November 5, 1998.
2. Block, M. R., telephone interview, October 19, 1998.
3. Cochin, T. J., Continuously Improving Your Environmental Strategies, *Corporate Environmental Strategy,* 2(57), 1998.
4. Ibid.
5. Bailey, telephone interview.
6. Jackson, S. L., telephone interview, November 18, 1998.
7. Summary Table of Economic Benefits, Excel Partnership, Inc.'s Implementing an ISO 14001 EMS training course.
8. Schell, D., The Greening of Wilton Armetale: Pennsylvania's First Environmentally Friendly Foundry Offers Model, *International Environmental Systems Update,* 3(12), 1997.
9. Schell, D. J., telephone interview, January 7, 1999.
10. Corporate Press Release, Ford Motor Company, December 8, 1998.
11. Ibid.
12. Ibid.
13. Ibid.
14. Porter, C. H., telephone interview, December 11, 1998.
15. Parry, P., Ford Motor Company Wins Environmental Performance Race with ISO 14000: First Automaker to Certify All Manufacturing Sites across the Globe, *International Environmental Systems Update,* 1(12), 1999.
16. Quisling, R. W., telephone interview, December 16, 1998.
17. Parry, *IESU,* p 12.
18. Ibid.
19. Environmental Report, Ford Motor Company, 8, 1998.
20. Ibid., pp. 12–14.
21. Letter to Business Partners, Bristol-Meyers Squibb, November 5, 1998.
22. Bristol-Meyers Squibb Environmental, Health and Safety Requirements for Contractors and Suppliers — Frequently Asked Questions, p. 1.
23. Nagle, G., telephone interview, January 6, 1999.
24. Web site, Bristol-Meyers Squibb, http://www.bms.com.
25. Ibid.
26. Ibid.
27. Parry, P., Bristol-Meyers Squibb Joins Ranks of Companies Seeking to Green Its Worldwide Supply Chain, *International Environmental Systems Update,* 1(1), 1999.

28. Ibid.
29. Environmental Health & Safety Performance Report, Baxter International, Inc., 1998.
30. Doll, J., Meeting and Beating ISO 14001?: Baxter International Claims Integrated System Is Better, If Not 'BEHSt,' *International Environmental Systems Update,* 8(9), 1998.
31. Ibid.
32. Tusa, W., telephone interview, September 15, 1998.
33. *What Is Your Share of $130 Billion?* Brochure, U.S. Environmental Protection Agency, 1998.
34. Ibid.

Chapter 4

Case Studies

As the author has investigated implementation stories across the country since 1996, she has discovered many fascinating dimensions of ISO 14001. But a predominant one is that ISO 14001 standard writers accomplished most of what they set out to do. They wanted a standard that would provide all companies — despite their size or industry sector — with the specifications for implementing an effective environmental management system (EMS). They wanted a flexible framework that would allow corporations to adapt the standard to their needs. Whether the company is a three-person, family-owned dairy business or a multinational corporation that manufactures spy planes, ISO 14001 was designed to suit the company's needs. To foster that flexibility, the standard does not require certification but allows for a company to self-declare conformance to the standard — an option not available under the ISO 9000 quality management system.

ISO 14001 has its critics — those who say the standard has holes in it. The author agrees the standard can be improved through a clarification of some of the language, but that is why the International Organization for Standardization has a revisions process in which standards are revised on a typical five-year cycle. When ISO Technical Committee 207 formally revises the standard, there's no doubt that some improvements will be made. But from this writer's standpoint, the members of Subcommittee 1 who drafted the standard accomplished exactly what they set out to do — publish a standard that is adaptable for a multitude of potential users.

To demonstrate ISO 14001 versatility, the author highlights the implementation experience of a small, 5000-student university, a large tools and equipment developer, an automobile manufacturer, the U.S. Postal Service, and one of the world's leading technology companies. In each case, ISO 14001 was stretched to meet the unique needs of its diverse users. And it met the test.

The University of Missouri — Rolla

Established in 1870 as the first engineering school West of the Mississippi, the University of Missouri – Rolla (UMR) "has virtually written the book on education in science and engineering" with programs designed to prepare students for life beyond the classroom.[1] And that's just one reason why the university has decided to pursue certification to ISO 14001 — to make that publicity slogan a reality.

Ranked in the top 20 in engineering degrees awarded annually, UMR began as the Missouri School of Mines and Metallurgy before becoming one of four universities in the Missouri system. The school offers degrees in engineering management, management systems, aerospace engineering, ceramic engineering, chemical engineering, chemistry, electrical engineering, mechanical engineering, metallurgical engineering, mining engineering, nuclear engineering, and much more. To provide a quality education for these students and to help professors with research, UMR handles more chemicals than most state universities. The school decided to pursue ISO 14001 as a means of managing the chemical use and to provide students a real-life laboratory because, once they enter various industry fields, knowledge of the international environmental management system standard will give them a competitive edge.

"Our thought was that when any chemical gets to the campus we would be able to track it — to where it is, what room it is in, what professor is using it, what amount is left, until it becomes part of the waste and we can really add it to the particular waste manifest," said Mohammad "Mo" Qayoumi, vice chancellor for administrative services at UMR.[2]

"We saw a number of advantages," he continued. "First of all, we have a legal and moral responsibility for the safety of our students, staff, and faculty who are working around chemicals to know where the chemicals are, what kind of danger they may be exposed to, and how we are taking care of those dangers to minimize them. So, that was the number-one issue. Second, and a very important one, (we wanted to be in better) compliance with the law. ... Third, if we adopt a more preventive approach, in the long run the business cost is going to be far less than (if we take) the reactive approach."

Qayoumi also saw a tremendous marketing advantage to ISO 14001. "If our students who end up working in industry are more familiar with an internationally recognized standard like ISO that is part of their curriculum, then when they are out in industry that makes them more marketable. They will be far more employable by having that information."

For example, Qayoumi said no matter how much a pilot logs time on a simulator, there's no substitute for actual flight time. The real test is in the cockpit. So, UMR wants its students to learn how to handle chemicals well and to be aware of what ISO 14001 can do for them.

"If we teach them the proper safety and the standards that they would be expected to know in industry, that will make them that much more valuable to industry."

Qayoumi came to the Rolla campus, which is about two hours west of St. Louis, in December 1995, and he saw some environmental issues he thought needed to be addressed. In the past, UMR had been fined, so the university worked with the Environmental Protection Agency on consent agreements to work off the school's obligations. One of the school's biggest consent agreements, he said, was the establishment of a major chemical tracking system. The school would like to be able to track its chemical usage in much the same way Federal Express tracks its packages, he said. University officials took a step back and looked at the broad picture. "We have so many different departments that deal with chemicals, this is such a core part of our activity that we cannot really look the other way," Qayoumi said. So, they began to look at ways to be proactive rather than reactive, he said, noting this was around the time ISO 14001 was published in September 1996.

After examining the new standard, UMR decided to implement ISO 14001, and he hopes the university will be certified by a third-party assessor. But a certification process for any bureaucracy as steeped in tradition as a university presents a few more challenges than the average company, he said. "Universities are run by tradition rather than rules and regulation," he said. "When a CEO tells a company to implement ISO 14001, the company has to do it. Industry is far more hierarchical. When a decision is made from on top, compliance is expected from everybody in an organization. In a university, that requires a lot more finesse; it requires a lot more negotiation. You have people who are used to one type of work habit, and they've been around chemicals for 40 or 50 years, and then you ask them to change some of their practices, so it will take a bit more work than what people have to do in industry.

"For us the challenge is more of a change-management issue."

Another challenge is the mere cost of implementing ISO 14001, he said. According to materials supplied by UMR, ISO 14001 certification has three main cost factors. First, the cost of the third-party registrar; the initial certification audit for UMR has been estimated between $80,000 and $100,000, with the subsequent annual surveillance audits coming at a price tag between $20,000 and $30,000. Second, the cost of employee time will be substantial. Third, additional resources will be needed to set up new procedures and organizational structures.

"It's one of those things where we ask ourselves: Do we want to pay now or 10 times more later?" he said, adding that cost and tradition were the only two disadvantages of pursuing certification.

UMR's certification process will take a total of three years because of the complexity of the university setting as compared to a company. For example, most industries might deal with large amounts of chemicals within a small spectrum of chemicals, but UMR handles smaller amounts of chemicals within a gigantic spectrum of options. "Universities in that sense are more like Noah's Ark — we have a little bit of everything," he said.

Also, the chemicals used by professors on various research grants may change every year or two, adding to the challenge.

One requirement of ISO 14001 is that every employee is aware of the environmental program and policy statement. UMR wants all of its employees, faculty, and students to be trained, he said, noting that attrition, graduation, and in-coming freshmen every year make it difficult. Qayoumi said the school is looking at computer-based training as the best method of reaching so many different people — about 1000 new people every year on the 5000-student campus.

Qayoumi added that UMR's certification efforts are somewhat unique because he knows of only a handful of other universities exploring ISO 14001. But he quickly added that he has not been actively trying to find out what other schools are pursuing this, and there might be more. Noting ISO 14001 certification would be difficult at large universities, he said UMR's size makes the goal achievable. And just like industry, without strong support from the very top, these efforts could not succeed. The chancellor, vice chancellors, deans, department chairs, and others have all been behind the ISO 14001 efforts.

"Rolla sees this as a very good business decision."

[In keeping with the journalistic practice of full disclosure, the author is a native of Rolla, Missouri, and she attended UMR for one year. Her father is associate professor emeritus at the school, where he taught for 21 years and then became UMR's registrar for an additional 16 years of service.]

Snap-on, Inc.

Snap-on, Inc. is a $1.7 billion global developer, manufacturer, and distributor of tools and equipment, according to the company's web site. Product lines include hand and power tools, diagnostics and shop equipment, tool storage products, diagnostics software, and more. And the company is pursuing corporatewide self-declaration to ISO 14001 at its more than 40 facilities.

Hiram J. Buffington, director of industrial & environmental services at Snap-on, said the company had an environmental management system long before ISO 14001 was unveiled, but because it is an international company, Snap-on wanted to pursue the model recognized around the world. "What we did was substitute one system for another or to put it into a different format," he said. "We did a side-by-side comparison in 1994 with our system and BS 7750, which was a forerunner of ISO 14001. Then in 1995, we converted our system into the Draft International Standard (DIS) 14001 format."[3] Snap-on's first seven facilities were audited against the DIS, and then when the final standard was published in September 1996, the facilities had their systems audited against the final standard. Buffington quickly clarified that these audits were internal since the company was self-declaring conformance to the standard rather than going through a third-party certification process. But to add weight to the internal auditing program, Snap-on sent two of its employees to auditor training, and they both received certification through an accredited course, he said.

Snap-on has a commitment that all of its facilities worldwide will become self-declared to the standard, Buffington said, noting that the company will not seek third-party certification unless the marketplace requires it. He said he handles the calls from other large companies inquiring about Snap-on's EMSs practices. He usually sends them the *Environmental, Hygiene & Safety Management System Manual of Practice* outlining its procedures and that satisfies the potential customers, he said. So, at this point, Snap-on can see no market-driven reason to seek third-party registration, he noted.

Buffington said another reason senior management decided to pursue self-declaration rather than certification is that Snap-on did not reap the anticipated business benefits of third-party registration with ISO 9000. He said the company invested a lot of money and did not see the returns that were expected. "Maybe had ISO 14001 come along first, we would have done the third-party registration," he said, noting the self-declaration option of ISO 14001 is not available under ISO 9000.

Snap-on spends about half a million dollars annually for the administrative costs of its worldwide ISO 14001 program. Those costs cover training, records retention, and increased documentation. "We thought it [ISO 14001] was as good as what we had before. We thought it is something that is going to catch on and be the standard throughout the world. I guess that's what we get for that extra half million dollars a year. Now this conforms with a system that is probably going to be recognized in every country around the world. So that is what we get for our $500,000."

Naming some of the other business benefits of ISO 14001, Buffington said they include reducing or eliminating "unplanned compliance costs" and cost savings due to efficiency and improved processes. The ISO 14001 program also has enhanced the training efforts at the company. Buffington said Snap-on had training initiatives in place, but with the internal audits, the training has been bolstered.

"Our decision was that we believe in being proactive on the environment," Buffington said. "We had a system in place. We did an analysis, determined it was not a very big step for us to move over and lay this into this new format, and it had good probability of being accepted around the world. And we just think it makes business sense to do that next step."

Getting Good Help

A good consultant means — not everything — but just about. At least that's the implementation experience of Lee A. Sanders, the environmental coordinator for Honda Transmission Manufacturing (HTM) in Russells Point, Ohio. HTM earned its ISO 14001 certificate on June 8, 1998, becoming the first Honda plant in North America to achieve that goal. Honda Motor Co. has committed its plants worldwide to becoming ISO 14001 certified by December 1999.[4] While Sanders was glad HTM was the first Honda plant in North America to earn a certificate, she said the journey was not as smooth as it should have been.

The biggest mistake HTM made in implementing the ISO 14001 EMS was in the first consultant the company hired, she said, declining to name the consultant for confidentiality purposes. She said HTM selected a well-known consultant based on the person's reputation, put trust in the consultant's advice, and Sanders found herself having to backtrack and start over with a new consultant. If an environmental manager hires someone to help with implementation, make sure the person knows what he or she is talking about, she advised others who might be following in HTM's footsteps. Reputation alone does not cut it, she said, adding that companies should ask for a demonstration of the consultant's work and references.[5]

But despite a rocky start, Sanders had other major factors weighed in her favor. First, she did not have to persuade top management to swallow ISO 14001. No, the Honda commitment to the international voluntary standard actually came from the top when the president of the company gave a speech in late 1996 that was designed to usher in the new year. In this speech, he declared that Honda was going to step up its environmental initiatives. Second, the employees embraced the program and made it their own.

In an HTM press release, the company outlined some of the benefits it gleaned from earning its ISO 14001 certification:

- Environmental management becomes a corporate priority that is recognized in every area of operation.
- An EMS provides integrated management, bringing all functions into the system.
- ISO 14001 involves the entire company in the process of continual improvement.
- Associates' training allows them to be more environmentally responsible.
- Contractors and suppliers are required to improve their systems.
- Emergency response plans prepare the facility to handle any significant hazard that may arise.
- Open communication with employees and the public about the environmental aspects of the plant.
- The company will continue an ongoing assessment of environmental performance.[6]

When HTM began its ISO 14001 journey, there was not much information available, she said, noting that she has learned that keeping the program simple is a good way to ensure employee involvement. The crux of ISO 14001 is that a company must say what it is going to do and then do it. So when companies write their environmental policy, objectives and targets, and procedures, they should keep them as basic as possible, knowing that one word can change the meaning of what they will have to do to be in conformance to the system.

Going Postal Means Going Green

It never fails: when Dennis Baca talks to people in the private sector, they are always perplexed that the U.S. Postal Service (USPS) has an aggressive environmental program. What could the Postal Service possibly have to do with the environment? Plenty.

Baca, manager, environmental management policy at the USPS headquarters in Washington, D.C., said that people think about their local postal office when they think about the Postal Service and they just can't connect the two. But his nonpostal friends begin to understand why the USPS is so concerned about the environment after Baca explains to them about the potential impacts. The USPS has 38,000 facilities, with 200,000 vehicles making deliveries 302 days out of the year, and 800,000 employees. Because of the Postal Service's size and potential impact on the environment, Baca said, "We should be demonstrating good corporate citizenship in relation to the environment."[7]

Like a good politician, Baca said he is aware that in the 21st century the top three issues will be Social Security, health care, and the environment, with the latter two being linked.

Adding a second observation from his encounters in the private sector, Baca said that often people complain that the Postal Service is responsible for the junk mail in landfills. But the Postal Service is a transportation and delivery system and should not be held responsible for the junk mail generated by companies that are advertising through direct mail. Baca said there are 42 million address changes every year, and much of that advertising mail is not forwardable. So, the USPS tries to find recycling facilities to take the mailers to avoid overflowing the landfills, he said.

More than 180 billion pieces of mail are collected, transported, processed, and delivered every year, according to the web site of the USPS. And that enormous undertaking requires a great deal of energy — both the human kind and the expenditure of natural resources such as fuel to run the delivery trucks and vans. As a result, the Postal Service has dedicated itself to an aggressive environmental program that makes its facilities better places to work and reduces their impact on the environment. In 1993, the USPS initiated an effort to integrate environmental decisions into daily business operations, drawing up a set of Seven Environmental Guiding Principles and an Environmental Strategic Plan. The seven principles involve a commitment to:

- Meet or exceed all applicable environmental laws and regulations in a cost-effective manner;
- Incorporate environmental considerations into business planning;

- Support the sustainable use of natural resources by promoting pollution prevention, waste reduction, recycling, and reuse of materials;
- Expect every employee to take ownership and responsibility for environmental objectives;
- Work with customers to address mutual environmental concerns;
- Measure progress in protecting the environment; and
- Encourage suppliers, vendors, and contractors to comply with similar environmental protection policies.[8]

According to statistics available on the USPS web site, these environmental initiatives have reaped tremendous results to date. The USPS recycled about one million tons of material, resulting in $8 million in 1997 alone. The White House has given the Postal Service 27 Closing the Circle Awards since 1995 for its recycling achievements. The USPS also has cut its energy usage by about ten percent since 1991. Participating in the U.S. Environmental Protection Agency's Energy Star® program, the USPS has committed to replace 15,000 exit signs in post offices across the country with ones that are more energy efficient. In the area of vehicle fleet management, the USPS also has begun to use alternative fuels, re-refined oil, and retreaded tires.

"The United States Postal Service is committed to providing employees and customers with a safe and healthy environment," according to a USPS statement on the Web. "Environmental protection is the responsible thing to do and makes for sound business practices."[9]

Along with its corporate environmental initiatives, the USPS also is dabbling in ISO 14001. John H. Bridges, III, area environmental compliance coordinator for the Capital Metro Operations, is a member of the U.S. Technical Advisory Group (TAG) to Technical Committee 207 (TC 207), and he sees a compatibility between the EMS standard and the environmental efforts of the USPS. So, he was instrumental in getting an ISO 14001 pilot project off the ground.

"We put together a proposal about a year ago to look at how we can complement our environmental programs using the ISO 14001 process," Bridges said in October 1998.[10] "And we selected Gaithersburg, Maryland, as our test facility based on the employee involvement and the high morale. Basically, we saw some potential that if we want to make this work, it could work at many of our facilities. The facility is not our largest," but it was a good choice for the pilot because of the employees. Bridges said the Gaithersburg employees wrote the environmental policy themselves, and then the plant manager signed it. The more than 1000 employees feel a part of this process because they are attending the meetings, seeing what is happening, and it's their program, said Bridges, who participates on the Environmental Management Task Force of the President's Council on Sustainable Development. The USPS management wants to let the Gaithersburg employees really develop the ISO 14001 program so they will have ownership of it, he said.

The facility's ISO 14001 program will be linked into the overall USPS quality movement, called CustomerPerfect. The USPS has initiated a companywide environmental management system based on the CustomerPerfect philosophy. Baca described CustomerPerfect as the Postal Service's commitment to ensuring that everything it does meets or exceeds customer expectations in a businesslike manner that results in continued use of the Postal Service from a competitive standpoint. The USPS wants its customers to view it as a world-class provider of mail services. The USPS also is committed to the Malcolm Baldridge quality criteria. Bridges said he sees the pilot project and potential for other ISO 14001 activities as complementary to both of those efforts.

Bridges said the Capital Metro Operations evaluated its environmental programs and discovered they were not strategically aligned to the business, and through the EMS process they are aligning the core business processes and adding value to the bottom line. "I think if people look at their current operating infrastructure they have all the pieces there for an EMS. It's just bringing them all together through a standardized process for continuity and consistency," Bridges added.

Bridges said the ISO 14001 planning process helped the Gaithersburg facility realize that it didn't have many environmental procedures in a central location. "We didn't have good focus on a lot of our hazardous waste identification program, our record keeping. We had it, but in different areas, not centrally located. Some aspects (they discovered, include) not properly following our waste streams. Our pollution prevention plans really weren't tied back into procurement or acquisition, so we saw a different light. And the employees were actually able to visually see that what they do in their operations link back to somebody else in the organization."

He continued, "We are hoping to reduce the bottom line from some of the waste streams that are being generated there presently. We have been able to capture a better return on investment on some of our solid wastes that are going out to be able to recycle more of this material. I think the quality of life issues will certainly improve, because now the employees are more actively involved and can contribute to safety, environmental, health issues that impact them on a day-to-day basis. As well as reducing some of our chemical waste streams that were coming in previously."

For example, the five Capital Metro hubs have saved $150,000 in cost avoidance within 15 months through a recycling program. Large catalogs and other materials are shipped to the hubs on wooden pallets, and each of the facilities was spending between $20,000 to $30,000 a year for disposal of those pallets. Capital Metro signed an agreement with another agency that picks up the pallets for free and reuses them for shipment. That same agency even reuses the broken and or seemingly unusable pallets by collecting them and turning them into mulch.

Bridges added that he hopes the success of the Gaithersburg facility will easily transfer to other postal facilities.

Baca said he thinks the Postal Service's ISO 14001 activities make good business sense, because Europe and Asia are using ISO as their benchmark. "For us to compete and do business globally, we are going to have to understand and be responsive to those same standards."

Addressing the Gaithersburg pilot, Baca said he is pleased the facility used activities based costing (ABC) methods that integrate environmental and business decision making. "If we focus on the up-the-pipe approach rather than the end-of-pipe, we can reduce waste streams, increase energy efficiencies, and improve our bottom line."

Paul Fennewald, environmental programs analyst at the USPS headquarters environmental management policy, said the USPS environmental management system should reap tremendous benefits in reducing pollution. The Postal Service has an expansive transportation network. By rolling out the EMS procedures nationally, Fennewald said he hopes to greatly reduce the Postal Service's impact on the environment through the emissions of their vehicles.[11]

Another business driver that Fennewald identified was the improved organizational and employee effectiveness. For example, he said the USPS has about five or six employees at the corporate headquarters. "If I could get everyone here (at corporate) to do everything the same way (procedurally), then I will improve our efficiency six times," Fennewald said. "Now you say, okay, I have 10 or 11 areas, and if I have all the 11 areas doing it the same way, that's 66 times more efficient. ... It can be as simple as, how am I going to document something? Or how am I going to label something? How am I going to maintain files? If we can get that replicated, we really improve employees' effectiveness. Things are easier and quicker to do. That's an unknown benefit with transferability and trainability.

"My first challenge is to get the headquarters acting as a separate entity in the way we do business," he continued. "I'm not talking about robots using the same style. I'm talking about the same procedures and processes that we use. There's a direct tie back into our quality movement, which is process management, and the environment can benefit from all of that."

Fennewald said that with an EMS, companies can never simply say, "Here's a model, go use it; here's a standard, go use it," because EMSs involve a dynamic process. That process requires a periodic review in terms of how things are working, how the business is operating, and remaining current with process flows to ensure effectiveness.

"And so that is what we are building into our systems."

Noting that his background is in business administration, not the environment, Baca said he sees the Postal Service's environmental initiatives as "a better way of doing business for the short-term and in the long-term by ensuring that we reduce the waste streams at the front end and factor that into our decision-making processes that result in more stable rates for the postal purchasers."

He continued, "The Postal Service can be the business partner to the U.S. economy in the 21st century by maximizing our vehicle fleet and our network to reach every household on a daily basis, and reduce the number of trips individuals might have to make in a society that is becoming more and more technology-friendly. ... We are truly committed to sustainable development."

Lockheed Martin Corporation

Formed in March 1995, Lockheed Martin was the result of a merger of two of the world's technology companies — Lockheed Corporation and Martin Marietta Corporation. The next year, Lockheed Martin combined with the defense electronics and systems integration businesses of Loral Corporation, according to a brief history on the company's web site. The new company's vision involves becoming the world's leading technology and systems enterprise, and one component to achieving that goal is ISO 14001.

Lockheed Martin has developed its own Environmental, Safety, Health (ESH) Management System that is adapted from and very similar to ISO 14001. Because Lockheed Martin is committed to business unit self-governance, the corporation did not want to mandate certification on all of its facilities worldwide, said Stephen Evanoff, manager of Central Environment, Safety & Health Services.[12] The individual sites within Lockheed Martin are free to decide whether to pursue ISO 14001, and to date, the entire electronics sector, or 29 facilities in the United States, Canada, and the United Kingdom have earned ISO 14001 certificates. Also, one major aerospace plant has registered, a second had been recommended for registration by its auditor at the time of this writing and the certificate was expected within a short time, and one aerospace plant that works on top-secret defense systems has self-declared for security reasons.

"We wanted to get the goodness out of implementing the system but not require people to spend money to achieve certification to 14001," Evanoff said. "So what we ended up designing was a derivative of 14001 for environment, safety, and health. Rather than getting people hung up on aspects and impacts, we require that people do a traditional hazard identification, risk assessment, and prioritization of their resources based on risk. And then, of course, compliance is a little more strongly emphasized by way of corporate policy than it is in the standard. And we de-emphasize a lot of the more detailed documentation in the standard, because what we are really trying to do is get people to integrate environment, safety, and health, and then integrate ESH as a package into the business in a cost-effective way that manages business risk and ensures that they are giving compliance its proper attention."

But there are only minor distinctions, Evanoff said, noting that "anybody that implements our management system by way of corporate policy is pretty close to being set for registration."

Norman A. Varney, Jr., associate general counsel of the Environment, Safety, and Health for the Electronics Sector of Lockheed Martin, said the electronics sector is one of the larger subdivisions within the company and was created out of about 20 different corporate ancestries through the various mergers. These ancestries, ranging from General Electric to Honeywell, comprise 13 business units in nearly 30 facilities, so from an ESH standpoint, the new Electronics Sector had to harness a consistent approach to managing the environmental aspects of those varying businesses. So, the Electronics Sector needed a comprehensive EMS and decided in early 1997 that ISO 14001 was a good model, he said.[13]

"We also saw that environmental considerations were integral to business performance, things such as cost and productivity, among others," Varney said. "We realized that environmental issues are not manageable by a lean environmental staff alone. We needed to integrate environmental considerations into our overall business management."

Varney said when the Electronics Sector focused on ISO 14001, he had several expectations. First, he saw value in the standard because it was so adaptable. ISO 14001 provides a good baseline rigor and an approach that is open to a variety of cultures, processes, and businesses, he said. Businesses that had good but relatively informal management systems would find it an easy transition into ISO 14001, he said. And for those business that did not have a system, ISO 14001 would help them get up to par, he added. Second, Varney said Lockheed Martin saw the value in implementing and certifying to a standard that would become the globally recognized way of doing business. Third, the standard had practical application within the Electronics Sector. "We saw that it would allow us to distribute responsibility and ownership throughout our given business units," Varney said. "Everyone would end up being responsible for environmental aspects of his or her job, and thus help out the environmental staff, which was going to continue to be relatively lean. It allowed a proactive and integrated approach ... as opposed to a reactive or piecemeal approach."

Varney said Lockheed Martin also thought ISO 14001 would help the company from the standpoint of business performance and return on investment. "Among other things, we felt it would help us reduce our waste disposal and material procurement needs," Varney added. "It would help us reduce the number and scope of the permits we would need. Such results would help us sustain an effort to keep our ESH staffs relatively lean. All of which go to cost reductions and productivity enhancements."

Evanoff said the corporate drive toward an ISO-like ESH management system just made good business sense, and for the Lockheed Martin facilities that have opted to take the next step and earn certification, they will reap additional benefits. "It [the ISO-like system] has helped us be compliant more efficiently, and it also enabled us to continuously improve," Evanoff said.

But Evanoff and Varney both emphasized that Lockheed Martin did not base its decision to allow facilities to implement the standard on a simple business case argument. "In none of our discussions did we say, 'We're not going to do this unless we can show some very simplistic return on investment,' meaning we spent $40,000 to make some process changes and get a registration and I will get a simple payback of 12 or 16 months," Evanoff said. He said no one questioned the value or rationale of having an integrated management system for any area. "It seemed to us if you didn't have that basic management system you were at peril in terms of compliance and cost control and risk management. So we're expecting some return on investment in our compliance, efficiency, and in our ability to do business internationally. But I don't think anybody said, 'We won't do this unless we can show some immediate payoff.' And I think it will take us a couple years to try and quantify tangible benefits from this requirement."

He added, "I think the biggest benefits are going to come from smaller facilities and our smaller businesses that may have had a lot of the bits and pieces in place but they didn't have an integrated system. We forced everybody to think in systems terms."

Varney said that making "a business case" is a phrase open to interpretation. To him, a business case is not necessarily about showing that ISO 14001 saves X dollars. For Lockheed Martin, he said, it was a less tangible approach. Varney said it was simply a matter of pointing out to top management that "you manage finances; you manage legal efforts; you manage operations; you manage sales efforts; and you have a system for each. Why should you not have a system to manage your EHS responsibilities, given their breadth, risks, costs, and competitive impact? And why shouldn't it be managed like the other major functions as an integral part of the business? And that struck a chord. That simple concept really struck a chord. Well, the response was, 'Yeah, what is the system?' We didn't have a universal system or framework other than to be in compliance. And we felt we needed something better."

Varney said that in pursuing ISO 14001 registration, each of the businesses within the sector had the freedom to select its own registrar. This approach was taken for a couple reasons, Varney said. First, Lockheed Martin was on the cutting edge, pursuing ISO 14001 shortly after it had been approved as an American National Standard by the American National Standards Institute, thus virtually no registrar had practical experience or a performance record with the standard. Second, some of the businesses had an ISO 9000 certification and wanted to use the same registrar for their ISO 14001 endeavors, he said. Third, some of the businesses had a registrar preference based upon their international contracts in areas of the world where particular registrars were well-recognized and respected.

The Electronics Sector is seeing indications of customer preference for companies with EMSs, and ISO 14001 in particular. "We did have one business where getting a particular contract was dependent upon it being 14001-registered from a country in the Far East, the Pacific Rim," Varney said. "In another circumstance, a potential customer sent Lockheed Martin a questionnaire asking what management system it had or whether it had a formal EMS in place and, if so, to identify it."

One of Lockheed Martin's biggest customers is the U.S. Department of Defense (DoD), which has voiced much interest in ISO 14001 and has conducted a variety of pilot projects. The DoD has been interested in trading ISO 14001 implementation experiences with Lockheed Martin, Varney said. Although the DoD has not indicated it is a preference item in contracts that Lockheed Martin obtains from them, the EMS standard has been a topic of very positive conversations with the DoD, he said.

To date, Varney has been pleased with the adaptability of ISO 14001. Lockheed Martin manufactures everything from specialized computer chips to multiple rocket launching systems, and ISO 14001 has adapted to all of them, he said. The standard also has adapted to the service aspects of the company's business — everything from installing postal sorters to repairing avionics.

The cost of certification also was much better than the horror stories that one might hear in the marketplace, he said, noting that it was relatively inexpensive. For example, he said that on average a Lockheed Martin facility that had 6000 employees would spend between $35,000 and $50,000, including about 40 to 230 person-days implementing the system. But he quickly added that the cost is dependent on a variety of factors, such as the quality of a company's existing system and the corporate culture. If a company's culture is open to change and doing things in a better way, then the implementation is smoother, he said. "We also found that our large facilities tended to have good, existing EMSs, so they found it easier and relatively less expensive, whereas our smaller facilities often had less developed EMSs. And they had a more expensive, relatively speaking, effort to undertake," Varney said.

Varney admitted that the certification costs he outlined seem low, but he said that reality might reflect the fact that Lockheed Martin's major facilities were well down the road to having a good management system and this represented an "up-tick as far as the cost and time demands are involved." His cost figures include the cost of the registrar and the internal costs of training, documentation, the aspects and impacts analysis, and establishing the targets and objectives. Varney added that he is talking about facilities with 5000 to 6000 people as compared to a huge company like Ford Motor Company that might have several times that number at a particular site. Some larger companies obviously may have higher certification costs, he added.

Evanoff, who was one of 40 individuals worldwide recognized in 1997 by the U.S. Environmental Protection Agency for his work on replacing ozone-depleting solvents at an Air Force plant, echoed Varney.[14] For some companies, the biggest ISO 14001 expense is related to closing the gaps discovered through the gap analysis. Because Lockheed Martin already had largely shut those gaps down, the ISO 14001 implementation was smoother and cheaper.

Varney noted that the sector's benefits derived from ISO 14001 are anecdotal at this point. For instance, the corporate organization and each business audit the individual facilities, and the company has found a tremendous improvement in audit performance since "we undertook the 14001 program," Varney said. "Now, can I say there is a direct cause and effect? I can't. But do I believe there is one? Yeah. Because there is such a substantial change in mindset, people are including ESH considerations in doing their jobs, all the way down to the employee-line level, and as a result, performance as reflected in the audits is very much improved.

Not that it was bad to begin with, but it has just become especially good since then."

"We also feel our environmental performance has improved," he said, noting they've seen a reduction in the number of permits they need due to reduced emissions. For instance, Varney offered, one of the facilities is moving from large quantity generator status to small quantity generator reflecting better management of its hazardous waste generation. As far as business performance and return on investment, they are seeing some cost reductions due to reduced regulatory applicability, he said.

"We believe we are seeing a combination of cost reductions and enhanced productivity, reduced energy, water, and material needs, and then, of course, some potential for contract awards as a result of customer preference for having 14001."

In addition to the 29 facilities within the Electronics Sector, three major aerospace plants have pursued ISO 14001 — Lockheed Martin Astronautics in Littleton, Colorado; Lockheed Martin Tactical Aircraft Systems in Fort Worth, Texas; and Lockheed Martin Skunk Works in Palmdale, California. Evanoff said the first site is certified to the standard, the second site had been recommended for registration at the time of this writing in April 1999, and the Skunk Works facility chose to self-declare conformance to the standard. That unique facility manufactures spy planes, classified planes like the stealth fighter, and does work for the National Aeronautics and Space Administration (NASA). Skunk Works does not have a customer with a burning desire for the plant to be ISO 14001 registered, or any international or commercial business drivers for registration, but the site wanted to pursue the management system while maintaining the confidentiality of its top-secret work. So, the facility decided self-declaration provided it the flexibility to pursue the system and maintain customer confidentiality by not allowing third-party assessors access to the plant.

Because of the top-secret nature of the Skunk Works facility, "it would be fairly impractical for someone, a third-party, to come in and be able to properly assess the facility as to whether it met 14001 requirements," Varney added.

Lockheed Martin Tactical Aircraft Systems

Lockheed Martin Tactical Aircraft Systems has produced more than 7000 airplanes since the factory opened in April 1942, including the B-24, B-32, B-36, B-58, F-111, and F-16.[15] The U.S. Air Force plant sprawls across 725 acres and has buildings totaling 7 million square feet.[16] William C. Rosenthal, the company's environmental manager, said the plant decided to pursue ISO 14001 certification because of the business drivers associated with selling products in an international market. "We are a strong believer in the ISO 9000 standard and are registered to that standard," Rosenthal said. "We felt that ISO 14001 was a natural follow-up to that. We hoped to enhance our position in the international market and, quite frankly, we want to improve our competitive position in any way we can."[17]

Lance Lamberton, senior communications specialist, added that another reason the plant pursued ISO 14001 was for the enhanced corporate image. "I think there are some elements that you cannot quantify, but certainly the overall image of the company as being a responsible corporate citizen in the area of environment, health, and safety is the general perception we want to convey about the company."[18]

Rosenthal and Lamberton said that this business unit within Lockheed Martin also did not build the dollars-and-cents business case. "We did a business case, but it was not based on cost savings," Rosenthal noted. He said that the plant's predecessor company — prior to the mergers — was General Dynamics, and in 1984 that company made a strategic decision to establish a goal of achieving zero discharge for hazardous waste. That decision was the result of very strong feelings about liabilities and strategic considerations surrounding environmental issues in the mid-1980s, he said. "We kind of parlayed that into what we consider to be a very successful pollution prevention program at this company that is now Lockheed Martin Tactical Aircraft Systems, and that culture has kind of stuck. It is a pollution prevention culture. It is not to say that there is not more that we can do because part of the ISO 14001 approach is for continual improvement. But we have made significant reductions before we even got into the ISO 14001 mode of operations." For example, he said the plant's Toxic Release Inventory (TRI) releases and transfers have been slashed 99.4 percent since 1987.

According to a chart supplied by Lockheed Martin Tactical Aircraft Systems, the plant has made other significant strides:

- 100 percent reduction in PCB devices since 1984;
- 100 percent removal or replacement of underground tanks since 1984;
- 99.9 percent reduction in the use of Ozone Depleting Compounds (ODC) since 1987;
- 99 percent reduction in EPA 17 Compounds (1985) since 1988;
- 98 percent reduction in effluent heavy metal discharges since 1987;
- 97 percent reduction in Volatile Organic Compounds (VOC) air emissions since 1986;
- 94 percent reduction in manifested waste since 1984;

- 56 percent recycling of Nonhazardous Industrial Solid Waste in 1998; and
- 41 percent reduction in Nonhazardous Industrial Solid Waste Generation since 1991; all of those reductions translate into cost savings for the plant's bottom line.

Rosenthal said he is particularly proud that the plant had rid itself of its ODC use because, in 1992, a national newspaper article listed the plant as the largest emitter of ODCs among all military production facilities — a distinction the plant did not want. Prior to the publication of the article, the plant had been researching alternatives to ODCs and has been able to get out of that business, he said.

So, Tactical Aircraft Systems was already doing many of the things that ISO 14001 is intended to accomplish, Rosenthal said. But he thought that ISO 14001 would give the plant another opportunity to evaluate its processes and systems and perhaps to enhance employee awareness. The ISO 14001 certificate was "like recognizing what we have already done," Lamberton said. "… we are already doing all of this, and there is a standard out there we can pretty much meet."

Additionally, Rosenthal and Lamberton said that being ISO 14001 certified gives the plant a competitive edge in a highly competitive market. "I would describe it as a competitive discriminator," Lamberton said. "It necessarily gives us an advantage because it is one of many things that we bring to the table when we compete in the international market for sales of our aircraft. It is one of many factors that we want to put together to make us the supplier of choice."

Rosenthal said another business benefit has been the awareness raised with employees that has prompted tremendous input. As the more than 10,000 employees are exposed to the ISO 14001 program, they raise great questions and suggest ideas. "It is really interesting that we are hearing from people that we have never heard from before," Rosenthal said. "That is one that I had not expected." Despite having an existing system with a thorough internal auditing program, ISO 14001 has helped the plant identify processes and procedures that were not working as well as they had thought. "It is helping us discover areas where we can actually improve our processes," he said. "As we improve these processes, we are going to see these cost benefits that people are looking for. I cannot put a dollar value on all the pollution prevention success that we have had in the past because that was not what we were measuring. We were not measuring dollars; we were going after zero discharge, and the strategic leadership back in 1984 did not ask us to go out and save money. They asked us to go out and achieve zero discharge. They were looking at down-the-road liabilities, not short-term costs. It is pretty difficult to put a dollar sign on it. We do know that it is worth a whole bunch of money."

But he can assign some dollars to illustrate what he means by "a whole bunch of money." For example, Rosenthal said they know how much hazardous waste they were generating and what it cost to dispose of it. He estimated that by eliminating just that disposal cost alone, the plant saved $35 million, and that is an aggregate. "When I say that, I almost hate to mention the number because it is almost trivial to the total cost savings. ... So, $35 million is probably an order of magnitude lower than the actual savings, and that is just talking about the hazardous waste reduction," Rosenthal said. For example, he said the paint the plant uses on airplanes is very expensive, and previously the facility was throwing away the unused portions of the materials — the expense of the materials far outweighs that of the hazardous waste disposal, he said.

Lockheed Martin Tactical Aircraft Systems did a value engineering study on one project — the plant has implemented more than 80 projects that Rosenthal loosely defines as pollution prevention initiatives. But the value engineering study focused on the plant's project to eliminate its ODC use. The plant's engineers developed and patented a new solvent blend that is now used internationally. The blend reduced the vapor pressure of the solvent from a very high-vapor pressure to a very low-vapor pressure. So, the solvent did not evaporate and release into the air. After retraining the work force to use this new solvent, the plant analyzed what was spent and realized that the project saved $8 million over a five-year period.

Rosenthal also has a shorthand list, spanning 11 pages, of all the pollution prevention projects the plant has completed, and he supplied it to the author. The following are some of the highlights:

- In one project, the plant segregated secondary containment around tanks full of incompatible compounds, which if commingled meant they would cease to be useable. By minimizing the accidental mixing of these materials, the facility also reduced the need to dispose of them.
- The facility also managed to achieve a 100 percent reduction in the use of methylene chloride for cleaning metal fasteners. Instead, the employees initiated a cleaning process that used a device to mechanically agitate and clean the parts, eliminating the need for solvents.
- In another project, the facility achieved a 100 percent reduction in solvent blends containing perchloroethylene and methylene chloride, substituting water-based cleaners and low-vapor pressure solvents.

- The plant worked out a program with the local paper recycler to collect and recycle all telephone books. A similar project involved securing a paper recycler to collect and recycle white office paper. In another project, the plant sends all used oil filters to an off-site recycling facility, where the whole filter is recycled.
- Also, hydraulic oil is recycled on-site and returned directly to the point of origin.
- The facility also contracted with local firms to recycle oil and antifreeze for reuse in the marketplace. That project resulted in a 50 percent reduction in used oil manifested off-site for disposal.
- In another project, fewer tires are making it to landfills because of a recycling initiative. The used tires are recycled and used as raw materials for products or fuel rather than being shipped to the local landfill. In a similar case, scrap wood is being sent to a local composting facility rather than the landfill.

The pages of pollution prevention initiatives go on and on, and perhaps this explains why Lockheed Martin Tactical Aircraft Systems earned the corporation's ESH Excellence Award in 1996.[19] But that facility is not the only one within Lockheed to have its achievements honored. In September 1997, Lockheed Martin received the EPA's Best-of-the-Best Stratospheric Ozone Protection Award; only 15 corporations around the globe received this distinction.[20] In Lockheed Martin's newsletter, the *ESHReport,* the company highlighted some of its other ESH honors, such as the 1997 New York Governor's Waste Reduction and Recycling Achievement of Excellence Award for Lockheed Martin Federal Systems in Oswego, New York. Other honors include the 1998 EPA Green Lights Award for its Moorestown, New Jersey, site; the 1997 Department of Energy Pollution Prevention Award for "Return on Investment" at its Livermore, California, facility; and the 1998 Outstanding Achievement Award for Waste Minimization/Pollution Prevention from the Arkansas Environmental Federation — for the third year in a row.

Corporate Perspective

Evanoff said he is pleased with the progress of the company's ISO-like ESH management system, and he said one of the reasons the system has been so successful is that the corporation has developed a number of educational implementation tools. One of those tools is a brochure titled, "What Every Company President Needs to Know about Environment, Safety & Health Management Systems." This pocket-sized reference guide for senior managers includes the Lockheed Martin ESH ISO-like model, describing each element in simple, user-friendly terms (Figure 4.1). The brochure then describes the consequences of an ineffective ESH program, some of the common ESH challenges in operations, and some of the other ESH resources that corporate makes available to the individual business units. Those resources are available through the ESHWeb — a web site devoted to providing ESH resources such as guidance modules, all federal and state regulatory requirements, and training requirements. The web-based tools and services make sure that every Lockheed Martin facility can tap into the corporate resources, Evanoff said.

"Lockheed Martin senior managers can be justifiably proud of the impressive record of environment, safety, and health accomplishments our business units have compiled over the past several years," Peter B. Teets, Lockheed Martin's president and chief operating officer, said in the brochure. "To maintain momentum and remain an industry leader, we face the challenge of continuing to improve our ESH performance while reducing the cost of doing business."

Notes

1. You Are UMR, *Campus View Book,* University of Missouri-Rolla, 1998.
2. Qayoumi, M., telephone interview, November 6, 1998.
3. Buffington, H. J., telephone interview, October 29, 1998.
4. Corporate Press Release, Honda Transmissions Manufacturing of Russells Point, Ohio, July 9, 1998.
5. Sanders, L. A., telephone interview, September 17, 1998.
6. HTM Corporate Press Release.
7. Baca, D., telephone interview, April 5, 1999.
8. Postal Service web site.
9. Ibid.
10. Bridges, III, J., telephone interview, October 29, 1998.
11. Fennewald, Paul, telephone interview, November 16, 1998.
12. Evanoff, S., and Varney, N. A., conference telephone interview, December 22, 1998.
13. Ibid.
14. Best-of-the-Best in Ozone Protection, *EHS Report,* Lockheed Martin, 1(5), 1997.
15. Fact Sheet, Lockheed Martin Tactical Aircraft Systems, 1998.
16. Ibid.
17. Lamberton, L., and Rosenthal, W. C., conference telephone interview, January 6, 1999.
18. Ibid.

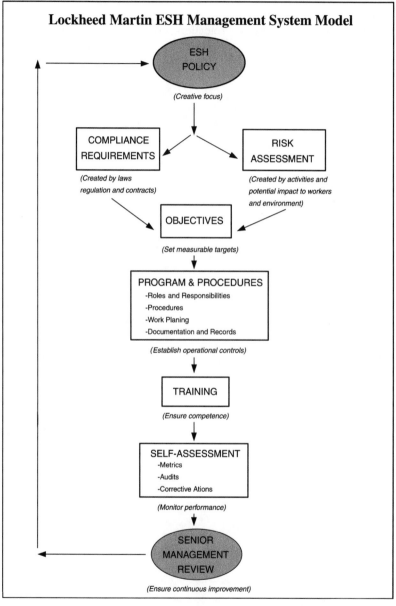

Lockheed Martin ESH Management System Model

ESH POLICY

(Creative focus)

COMPLIANCE REQUIREMENTS

(Created by laws regulation and contracts)

RISK ASSESSMENT

(Created by activities and potential impact to workers and environment)

OBJECTIVES

(Set measurable targets)

PROGRAM & PROCEDURES
-Roles and Responsibilities
-Procedures
-Work Planing
-Documentation and Records

(Establish operational controls)

TRAINING

(Ensure competence)

SELF-ASSESSMENT
-Metrics
-Audits
-Corrective Ations

(Monitor performance)

SENIOR MANAGEMENT REVIEW

(Ensure continuous improvement)

Source: From Lockheed Martin. With permission.

Figure 4.1

19. Hard Work and Results, *ESH Report: Special Report,* Lockheed Martin, 1(1), 1997.

20. Best-of-the-Best in Ozone Protection, *EHS Report,* Lockheed Martin, 1(5), 1997.

Chapter 5

Image Booster

ISO 14001 is not really supposed to be about public relations. The voluntary environmental management system (EMS) standard is designed to help companies manage their processes to minimize their impact on the environment. It's not really supposed to be a marketing tool, and some specialists say that it is not an actual driver behind most companies' decisions to implement the standard. But inevitably, public relations or an enhanced corporate image appears on almost everyone's list of business benefits of an ISO 14001 EMS. The good publicity a company receives for being environmentally proactive seems almost unavoidable — even if it is not the reason a company invests time and energy into changing its entire organization. But does this intangible, nebulous benefit have staying power? Or, in other words, does a company's ISO 14001 program bring it only fleeting recognition? The answers to those questions can be found in the organizations that have implemented ISO 14001, thereby forever changing their relationship to their communities. The answers can also be found in those companies that have turned their good neighbor reputation into a business advantage.

One such company is First Environment, Inc. of Riverdale, New Jersey, which was the first strategic management and environmental engineering firm in the United States to achieve ISO 14001 certification.[1] An environmental services company, First Environment pursued ISO 14001 primarily for the public relations or marketing value. First Environment helps its clients with an array of services, including implementation of the standard. So, it made business sense from a marketing standpoint for the company to have been through the same process that its clients faced.

"We can say, 'Been there, done that,' " said Reeva Schiffman, senior regulatory specialist at First Environment. "We can really go in and tell people about our real life experiences."[2]

Tod Delaney, First Environment president, said, "I think that for a small firm such as ours that is not terribly well known on a national basis, without having the ISO 14001 certificate, it would really be a complete barrier for us to enter into this market area of trying to help others with environmental management systems." Delaney said that very large consulting companies that compete with First Environment may not have an environmental management system from the standpoint of 14001, but they have a lot of people who may be capable or are able to compete in this field. "We never would be able to if we hadn't gotten our 14001 certificate. And what it does for us, on a case-by-case basis, is it levels the playing field with all the big guys."[3]

Schiffman added, "It even gives us a leg up very often."

She noted that sometimes potential clients are a bit skeptical of First Environment's certificate because the company is part of the service industry and they mistakenly think that means the company has no real impact on the environment. They wonder what potential environmental impacts First Environment could have, but as soon as Schiffman describes the company's activities in the field and its site investigation activities, they realize First Environment's system can be tweaked to fit companies within the industry. ISO 14001 is designed for use in both industry and the service fields, she said.

For example, Delaney said First Environment recently had secured a pollution prevention contract as a subcontractor to the U.S. Air Force — a new market for First Environment. As they began discussing how to set things up, Delaney said they realized that the company's EMS structure would help them run the contract. Having a written system helped them feel comfortable with this new market area.

"This helps us not only get contracts, but it helps us in executing work in new areas," said Delaney, who is a member of the U.S. Technical Advisory Group to Technical Committee 207.

Schiffman concurred, "It is basically a predeveloped framework for attacking every job. And you use different elements of it for different jobs depending on how complex they are. We have really begun to do some things more efficiently, so in terms of that we are wasting less time. We are saving staff time in terms of efficiency."

After implementing ISO 14001 at First Environment, Schiffman said that if she could point to one primary benefit of the EMS, it would be the implementation of the corrective and preventive action process. "There has been and continues to be cultural barriers to this — it is just the natural unwillingness to admit to having made a mistake," she said. "But we are trying to teach new tricks — basically that means that making a mistake is not bad unless you make the same one again. Or somebody else in the organization makes the exact same one, but there are always things to learn from projects and things to learn from mistakes and ways to do it better. This has become integral to the way we run all of our projects. We have a corrective-and-preventive-action system that crosses all lines. And it is not only related to environmental issues."

For example, First Environment completed a 735-site audit program for a chain of fast food restaurants located throughout the United States. The audits were completed successfully within the 60-day, client-imposed deadline. Although First Environment relied on processes previously developed, additional areas of friction were encountered that had been forgotten about or which arose from the larger scope of the project. At the completion of the project, pursuant to its internal project debriefing and the corrective-and-preventive-action process, the team met to identify the problems that occurred and analyze their causes so that the current process could be improved for the next project. The team debriefing process provided invaluable information applicable to other projects, which will result in greater efficiencies and cost savings.

Another major result of ISO 14001 implementation is enhanced training — because First Environment employees have been trained, they can more effectively talk to their clients about how to train their personnel.

Although ISO 14001 has helped First Environment's marketability, Schiffman said the company did not do an "official cost analysis" or try to build a business case based on waste minimization or cost savings. As a service industry, those cost savings are not as readily available, and trying to project new markets based on ISO 14001 certification was practically impossible. But the decision to pursue it, Delaney said, was nonetheless obvious. "We were looking at this as a business sector that we wanted to get into, and not having an EMS" would have hindered that endeavor.

But becoming certified was an expensive undertaking in terms of lost productivity or billable hours. Nine employees served on a steering committee for about one year, with a handful of those committee members devoting enormous time to it in the final three or four months leading up to the certification. Delaney said the organization had no procedures in place, so the staff was starting from ground zero. One person who is "potentially 100 percent billable on projects" worked on virtually nothing else but writing those procedures for three months. They both said it was hard to project what that cost First Environment, but it was an expensive investment of his time because he could not bill for any work. Also,

Delaney said that First Environment probably invested much more in-depth training of employees than the standard requires because it wanted its employees to be able to translate their experience to their clients.

Even though First Environment did not build a business case based on projected cost savings, the company has helped other organizations do so. Most of First Environment's clients have made an internal decision when they hire First Environment, but in a few cases, Schiffman said that, "We have gone to senior management and made a presentation to help them." So, how does one build a business case? "Dollars," she said, noting that the bottom line is how to persuade senior management. One quick way to save money, Delaney added, is by reducing energy consumption. Most organizations pay their electric bills without ever identifying their cost centers, he said. If they evaluate the power utilization processes they have within the facility and either change them or get rid of them, they can make themselves more profitable just by looking at where the power goes.

"It [ISO 14001] is not going to be an instant gratification," Delaney said. "What you do get back immediately is knowing where you are spending your money on environmental issues, because that comes out of going through your aspects and impacts and putting things together. Knowledge of your operation that you didn't have before then allows you to make good business decisions as to what to do."

And for First Environment, one of its best business decisions was to use ISO 14001 as cachet into new markets.

Community Relations: A Natural

Jack Bailey of Acushnet Rubber Company admitted the New Bedford, Massachusetts, company pursued ISO 14001 certification for the money, but its return on investment has been so much more than dollars. "It has been a door opener for us. We've gotten international recognition. ... We've gotten good positive press, good feedback from regulators," Bailey said.[4]

He continued, "In general, what it does for us, it does raise expectations in the neighborhood, but it forces our good neighbor policy. We sit with our backs on the Acushnet River and in front of our facility is a residential neighborhood. They want to be sure that we are going to be a good neighbor, and we are not going to be dumping toxins on people and having all kinds of problems that threaten their homes. We have a long history in the neighborhood, and I think we've built up a trust with the neighbors. This [ISO 14001] is one way to reinforce that trust."

Acushnet Rubber Company was founded in 1910, but its facilities have been in the neighborhood since the late 1800s. The company refurbished old mill facilities into three manufacturing plants with more than 1000 employees in New Bedford. Many Acushnet employees live within walking distance of the plant, so "there aren't any secrets about what we are doing here," Bailey said. "We can't promise that we're never going to have a problem here, but I think we have enough support in the neighborhood so that if we do have a problem, they will feel we will handle it properly. We have enough containment and contingency programs to prevent any real harm to the neighborhood."

Because of Acushnet's leadership in the ISO 14000 arena, Bailey often is sought as a public speaker or conference leader. One of his favorite stories about Acushnet's implementation experience involves one of the company's employees. He said sometimes people misunderstand and think that Acushnet pursued ISO 14001 so it could pronounce itself one of the greatest environmental companies going, he said, adding that is not what the certification means. Pointing to the employee, he said, "When our employees are audited by TUV Management Services regarding our policy, they are asked, 'What does the policy mean to you as a worker?', and it has boiled down to the response of our employee Tony Mello, who said, 'We are trying to obey the law and be good neighbors.' "

That's what ISO 14001 is all about, said Bailey, adding, "The strength of the program is with our people and their involvement. That's what makes it work for us. The building and equipment isn't new. What's new is the way we are interacting with our employees."

What's in a Name?

Perhaps no company has gotten better press from its ISO 14001 certification than SGS-Thomson Microelectronics, because it had the first site certified in the United States, and probably one of the first in the world. The company's Rancho Bernardo, California, site was certified to the Draft International Standard (DIS) version of ISO 14001 in February 1996.[5] And since that time, the global, independent semiconductor company has been the focus of case studies, news articles, conference sessions, and book chapters. In fact, SGS-Thomson was a model that Acushnet's Jack Bailey was watching as he asked his management to pursue the international EMS standard.

"Overall, the company has been recognized as an environmental steward for its dedication to the environment from the corporate level, and it may have helped us gain more brand name recognition," said Joe Hess, the site's health, safety, security, and environmental team leader. "I don't have any hard data for that, but there certainly has been (some recognition)."[6]

But Hess said that the public relations benefit may have been diminished somewhat because of the company's name change. In May 1998, SGS-Thomson Microelectronics became STMicroelectronics, the name the company is operating under now. But name change or not, this author believes STMicroelectronics is still the one everyone looks to as an ISO 14001 implementation example.

"Being first wasn't really a goal," Hess said. "It was a goal to do something and to get out there and show that we were leaders in the field."

Before ISO 14001 was published, the company pursued validation to the European Eco-Management and Audit Scheme (EMAS), earning it in November 1995. Three months later, the Rancho Bernardo site received its ISO 14001 certificate based on the DIS, and then had the certificate revalidated after the final standard was published in September 1996. According to materials on STMicroelectronics' web site, the company is most likely the only organization in the world to have all of its manufacturing sites registered to ISO 14001 and validated to EMAS.

"The company firmly believes that financial and ecological responsibility are compatible goals: caring for the environment is not only compatible with its ethics, but also gives it a competitive edge," according to a statement on the web site.

Still Not A Driver

Every company this author has interviewed for newsletters, magazines, and books has said the public relations benefit has translated into an enhanced image that has been good for business. But virtually none of them know how to quantify that in terms of annual savings or earnings. In fact, one straight-spoken, no-nonsense consultant said that despite the fact public relations is a bona fide benefit of implementing the system, it is still not a driver.

"It's not the reason my clients are doing it," said Marilyn R. Block, president of MRB Associates in Potomac, Maryland. "Many of them have not publicized the fact they are pursuing this. It's not a key consideration. If they get the positive PR out of it, that's nice, but it's not the reason they pursued it. And if they got no PR, they would still be pursuing it. My clients are pursuing it for waste minimization and cost savings. ...

They think it's the right thing to do, and they can see some financial benefit from doing the right thing."[7]

Another consultant, James Haklik, said the market value of an EMS is evident for global companies. "I think what I have seen is that it is a challenge in the United States since it is a voluntary system," said Haklik, president of Transformation Strategies in Phoenix, Arizona. "The benefits of ISO 14000 are primarily the benefits of good environmental management, except where ISO 14000 in the international market provides some value. I think that a lot of the benefit to the American companies is because they deal internationally with countries that are much more vigorous in their support of ISO 14000."[8]

In addition to market value, Haklik said the real public relations benefit of ISO 14001 involves avoiding a bad public image more than sporting a good one. In the court of public opinion, companies can lose more by being grossly negligent of the environment than they can win by being environmentally proactive, he said. "It seems like what we see is people who are known for having done bad things," he said, pointing to the devastating Exxon Valdez oil spill in 1989. "But there might be another company that has really been good, but I couldn't tell you who that would be. It seems like it is more avoidance of bad press, in my experience, than gaining the positive benefit from being environmentally conscious relative to ISO 14000. Of course, no one in America knows ISO 14000 anyway."

Haklik said that most Americans don't have any awareness of ISO 14000, so the company would have to use its certification as a promotional tool. "I think for the public to translate that into a buying decision is probably a pretty low priority from what I can see," continued Haklik, who maintains an outstanding ISO 14000 web site, www.trst.com. "When they are going to buy a product, they look at utility and price, and whether it is a well-known manufacturer. I am not sure how much they are actually researching into the environmental friendliness of that company." But again, Haklik said that the negative press can result in consumers dropping products through boycotts and other measures.

An NGO Perspective

While there's no doubt that companies are reaping some public relations benefits from ISO 14001 implementation, the very notion of publicizing the achievement can be controversial in ISO circles. Deborah Siefert Morrill, who represents multiple nongovernmental organizations (NGOs) involved in the U.S. Technical Advisory Group (TAG) to Technical Committee 207 (TC 207), said she's concerned about ISO 14001 as a publicity tool. "What are they telling the public? ... How can the public even begin to comprehend this very, very complex environmental approach to even ask a question of the companies?"[9]

Morrill, project manager on the NGO Initiative: ISO 14001 project, said she is concerned about the transparency of the standard — especially if companies are going to advertise certification to imply that they are meeting their environmental responsibilities. She emphasized that she sees great potential in ISO 14001, but that the standard should be revised to incorporate better external communication requirements.

"I think that it [ISO 14001] is really the most important direction for the future of environmentalism because of the fact that it helps to build a new culture within industry," said Morrill, staff attorney with Community Nutrition Institute in Washington, D.C. "And facilities and organizations, on a daily basis, will incorporate environmental awareness and management into their day-to-day operations. And if you have an ISO 14000 or a similar EMS that has as its targets and objectives this type of environmental performance, then you are going to address these needs on a daily basis as part of your system. And I think that is terribly exciting and holds huge amounts of potential. However, the problem is that under the current system ... you don't know what targets or objectives an organization is targeting unless it chooses to tell you, and I think that is dangerous."

To implement ISO 14001, an organization must set objectives and targets as part of its process of reducing the significant impacts identified during the rigorous aspects and impacts analysis. And most companies keep those targets and objectives close to the vest. Industry leaders balk at NGOs and others in the public sector who want a more public accounting of the industry's voluntary activities. Industry leaders usually counter that ISO 14001 is a voluntary standard designed to take the company beyond regulatory compliance, and that the initiation of a voluntary, proactive system ought to be enough to demonstrate a good faith effort. Many within industry also note that they are hesitant to reveal private, corporate information because of the litigious nature of U.S. society, and because they are afraid that their efforts somehow will be turned against them. In fact, industry leaders have expressed concern about the atmosphere of distrust from NGOs and the regulatory community when they are trying to implement a voluntary system.

"There is one way to make us, the NGOs and regulators, feel better, and that is to tell us what you are doing with your management system," said Morrill, who is also the director of policy and program development at the Environmental Quality Management Institute in Washington. "If we have to sit back and guess what you are doing with your management system, we are going to fall into our old stereotypes of what industry does based on our past experiences with industries. And they are not giving us any reason to think differently when they are once again going to hide what they are doing. It is real easy to make us feel better: tell us what you are doing.

"It is what you don't want to tell us that worries us. Yet you say, 'Don't worry. Trust us.' That is what happened before. Industry said, 'This is private property,' and lo and behold, Love Canal. So we can't take that position anymore. The regulators and the environmental organizations can't do it. We are asking them very nicely to be transparent. Just tell us what you are doing."

Morrill said she is worried the standard does not require companies to make information about EMS performance available to the public. Just because a company certifies and improves its management system doesn't mean that company will continue to improve its environmental performance, she said, adding a piece of paper is no guarantee of performance.

"Every ISO 14001-certified EMS is different and produces environmental performance on a spectrum from barely acceptable to exceptional. These differences are not reflected in the certificate. I would like to see the standard require that a company make public in some type of environmental statement about their targets and objectives and how they are performing relative to their EMS — especially if they are going to publish their certification," she said. "If companies are going to use ISO 14001 as an internal tool and not publicize it, then more power to them." But if companies use ISO 14001 certification as a publicity tool, then she thinks they have an obligation to explain to the public what that means. "What concerns me is when you have this official-looking seal that says ISO 14001 certification for 'environment' management systems that looks very similar to an eco-seal, and the public has been trained over the last 20 years to look for eco-seals as an indication of 'environmental' preferability. An ISO 14001 EMS certification seal advertised by a company can lead the public to believe their products are somehow greener than another product from a noncertified company — and that's not true."

Morrill is concerned because many of the companies that have earned certification in the United States had mature EMSs in place, making minor adjustments to get certified. These companies already were making good strides environmentally, she said, adding that if the standard remains as untransparent as it is now, they will have no incentive to push for improved performance. Industry representatives quickly point out that the standard itself calls for continual improvement and that the process of surveillance audits and recertification will keep them moving toward the goal of improved environmental performance.

"I think industry thinks the NGOs and the regulators are both looking to see that 14000 becomes some type of a compliance tool," she continued. "And that is not necessarily true. Our concern is that a company can be certified and be able to publicize this certification, yet not be in compliance. You do not have to be in compliance to be certified."

However, a noncompliant company publicizing a certified "environmental" management system may come across to the public as some "officially" endorsed good environmental actor when they are just the opposite. "Green washing" only helps the bad actors; not the good companies or the public — so why tolerate it?

And Morrill isn't alone in her concerns that publicity of ISO 14001 certification could mislead the public. On April 21, 1997, a new international NGO was initiated at a press conference held in conjunction with the Fifth Plenary of TC 207 in Kyoto, Japan. The organization, the Certification Monitoring Network (CMN), was established to look out for false advertising claims about products that have been certified under a variety of systems, including ISO 14001.[10] At the press conference, another NGO representative, William E. Mankin, told *International Environmental Systems Update* that misleading publicity could be a potentially significant problem. "I think it really is a huge potential problem that will increase as more people start using ISO 14000," said Mankin, director of the Global Forest Policy Project. "Just the fact that somebody is watching means some people will be more careful to be honest in their claims."[11]

The Geneva-based International Organization for Standardization (ISO) also is concerned about companies making false claims related to ISO 14000. In fact, the standards organization decided to publish a pamphlet to help companies avoid making such false claims. According to an ISO press release, "Publicizing your ISO 9000 or ISO 14000 certification" is designed to counteract at least three main practices:

- Appropriating or using the ISO logo, which is a trademark;
- Giving the false impression that ISO authorized the certificate — ISO is responsible for developing and publishing the standard, but independent registrars provide the certification services; and
- Giving the false impression that an ISO 14001 label signifies "green" products — ISO 14001 provides specifications for an environmental management system, but does not guarantee environmentally friendly products.

"Businesses and other organizations which have invested time, energy, and money to obtain an ISO 9000 or ISO 14000 certificate understandably wish to publicize their achievement," the ISO booklet acknowledges. "This leaflet aims to help ISO 9000 and ISO 14000 certificate holders avoid the pitfalls of false, misleading or confusing claims ... ."

The leaflet clarifies some terms, explains how ISO works, discusses some of the potentially confusing scenarios, and then offers some sample advertisements. The 1998 publication is free and available from the ISO Central Secretariat at central@iso.ch.

The ISO guidelines are good information, but greenwashing has the potential to occur anytime a company publicizes to an uninformed audience, Morrill added, even when those guidelines are followed. "Its the act of publicizing something that the public is not familiar with under an official-looking seal with no requirements for further information that is the threat."

Great Opportunities

Although the potential for false and misleading claims is great, many companies are publicizing their certificates in an appropriate manner. In fact, the ISO leaflet provides some good examples of how to advertise a corporation's certification. And the publicity of an ISO 14001 is one of the areas of biggest opportunities, said Wayne Tusa, president of Environmental Risk and Loss Control, Inc. in New York City. "It's really challenging being a business out there," he said, noting the diversity of constituencies from regulators to public interest groups that can make life difficult for businesses. "There are so many special interest groups that businesses are constantly negotiating with to operate on a day-to-day basis — particularly if they want to make any changes. Think about the distinction between a company that has a great image and a company that has a poor image. And think about the dollars that are expended by companies that are perceived by the community and the regulators as good neighbors as opposed to the dollars spent by those perceived not to be responsive to public needs. There are enormous differences — it affects more than the environmental compliance budget. It impacts all of the activities of the organization whether it is the cost of insurance, advertising, obtaining operating permits, etc."[12]

He continued, "Personally, I think that this is an area where there are the largest business opportunities, because almost everyone prefers positive environmental behavior. For example, a positive environmental image is perceived as good by employees. There are some anecdotal studies out there indicating that companies with progressive environmental programs have less turnover because they are perceived by their employees, their families, and the community as good places to work."

Similarly, many permitting battles are lost by companies that have poor public images, he said, adding that many firms are beginning to figure out that being perceived as a good neighbor is a tremendous day-to-day operating benefit. And finally, Tusa said that Wall Street is starting to take notice of companies that have good environmental records. Pointing to a newspaper article about Wall Street and environmentalism, Tusa said, "If you think about how Wall Street works, it makes sense. If there's a negative incident in the press, your stock value goes down, and if there's a positive incident, it goes up. So one of the largest business benefits an organization can get out of ISO 14001 is an improved public image."

Another consultant, Suzan L. Jackson of Excel Partnership in Sandy Hook, Connecticut, said the marketing and public relations benefit is more than an external activity — they also can be an internal driver. One of the best benefits of registration that few companies recognize is the internal benefit of motivating employees, she said. Given the nature of business and human nature, she said, often the only way to sustain a long-term commitment to an EMS is through the certification process.[13]

Admitting that not all markets are requiring registration, Jackson said the marketing benefit is diminished without the registration, because that is what gives companies the public recognition. "That external driver works as an internal motivator. So by being registered you're making a commitment — a long-term commitment to improving and maintaining your system. And without the registration, it could happen, but it is the rare company that makes that happen without the external driver (of the registrar)."

An Auditor's Perspective

Mary-Rose Nguyen, a lead auditor with Bureau Veritas Quality International (BVQI), makes her living conducting third-party registration audits, and she has audited multiple sites within dozens of companies. She agrees with Jackson that the registrar provides motivation for the company to continue on the right path, as well as lends credibility to the EMS effort through an outside verification of the system. Even though certification may not be required in certain markets yet, most people within ISO circles consider a third-party stamp of approval as having more credibility, she said.[14]

"There's a big difference between self-declaration and registration," she said. "It is the credibility issue." When BVQI talks with potential customers, she said, most companies don't think the registration cost is prohibitive when compared to the implementation price tag. "The cost really is not so much more if you divide over three years (the period between recertifications); it's peanuts compared to what they are paying for implementation," she said. "Companies are registering because of the credibility. We are there every six months or year, and we are helping them continue to improve. The surveillance audits help keep them on track. It's motivation."

Without naming specific clients, she said that her customers have reaped tremendous benefit from an enhanced corporate image. For some of the clients, ISO 14001 certification has brought them three things they needed in their communities: visibility, visibility, visibility. Having a higher and positive profile within the community has helped them, she added.

Offering some anecdotal evidence of the importance of having a good image, Nguyen said one summer she went to a client's facilities with her children in tow. She asked her client if they could take her children on a tour of the site while she conducted her audit. They took her children on a half-day tour and explained to them about the technical facility. At lunch time, she asked them what they had learned on their tour, and they began to recount word by word what the company was doing. Later, she talked to the employee who had been talking with her children, and the person repeated the information verbatim to what the children had told her. After that, her children spread the company's story everywhere they went, from other facilities to their school. That experience had an impact on her children and even helped raise environmental awareness when they shared the experience with their classmates at school, she said. That company's internal employee training really paid off.

Nguyen, a leader within the U.S. TAG, said another client's activities had the potential to build bridges within the community, but the company had not recognized the potential. She was at the facility, which manufactures batteries, and she noticed, through the window, turkeys on the company's property. When she asked about it, she was told that they had a turkey habitat on the property. For some inexplicable reason, the turkeys liked the grounds surrounding the plant, and the company decided to let them live there — a sign that the company has a sensitivity to the environment.

"After we looked at their aspects, we said you need to focus on the good things you are doing," she said. "You are talking about negative things you want to improve, but you don't talk about the positive ones."

Initially BVQI's only lead auditor, Nguyen said that the ISO 14001 benefits she has identified through her auditing experience are threefold. First, companies are more aware of what is going on internally, because they have incorporated the environment into the business strategy of the company. Second, ISO 14001 registration helps companies improve, not just from a system point of view, but from a financial point of view. Third, the company becomes system-driven and takes corrective actions much sooner, involving more people in the process.

Being a third-party certifier, she said she does not get into the pros and cons or take a position on whether certification is good or bad for companies. But because of her firsthand exposure to so many companies, "I am going to have my say in this," she said, adding that companies often will reap far more benefits than they anticipate, but the results are proportional to the amount of time and effort put into implementing the system. "You need to know what you are trying to achieve," she commented. "You may have benefits beyond your main goal, but it all starts with the top management commitment."

Notes

1. Parry, P., A First for First Environment: Strategic Management and Environmental Engineering Firm Sets ISO 14001 Pace in States, ***International Environmental Systems Update,*** 1(8), 1998.
2. Delaney, T., and Schiffman, R., telephone conference call, January 29, 1999.
3. Ibid.
4. Bailey, J., telephone interview, November 5, 1998.
5. SGS-Thomson Grabs Brass Ring with First 14001 US Certification, ***International Environmental Systems Update,*** 2(1), 1996.
6. Hess, J., telephone interview, March 18, 1999.
7. Block, M. R., telephone interview, October 19, 1998.
8. Haklik, J., telephone interview, January 7, 1999.
9. Siefert Morrill, D., telephone interview, January 11, 1999.
10. Certification Monitoring Network Launched in Kyoto: Not-for-Profit NGO to Provide Clearinghouse Mechanism for Keeping Marketers Honest, ***International Environmental Systems Update,*** 6(13), 1997.
11. Ibid.
12. Tusa, W., telephone interview, September, 15, 1998.
13. Jackson, S. L., telephone interview, November 18, 1998.
14. Nguyen, M. R., telephone interview, January 8, 1999.

Chapter 6

Regulatory Relief

Command-and-control. Those ominous words reflect a relationship in which one party tells another party what to do and has the power to ensure that it happens. Although it doesn't sound like a healthy relationship, that is the phrase used to describe the U.S. regulatory framework designed to keep in check industry's impact on the environment. Regulators at the U.S. Environmental Protection Agency in Washington, D.C., and in the various states carry out the regulatory laws enacted by Congress and state governments, while members of industry seek to ensure they are in compliance with those laws. Both the regulators and the regulated seek to work together to demonstrate compliance. Sometimes that relationship is contentious, and sometimes it is amicable. But the system ensures that the relationship is always adversarial — one group makes sure another group toes the line.

Also, a third party is added to the mix because the environmental nongovernmental organizations (ENGOs) keep an eye on both groups. ENGOs make sure that government is vigilant in its watchdog role over industry. In the past, some members of industry, such as those depicted in the John Travolta movie, *A Civil Action,* have acted with a reckless disregard and callous indifference toward the environment. ENGOs don't ever want to be caught napping while egregious violations go unpunished. Love Canal must never happen again because they trusted industry to do the right thing, the author inferred from an interview with one ENGO representative.

With all of this baggage and distrust in the system, it's no wonder that many people hoped ISO 14001 would point to a new and better way.

And it does. But too many people heaped unrealistic expectations on the specification standard in terms of how quickly that new path could be blazed. The heightened anticipation for the publication of ISO 14001 in September 1996 has led some to be frustrated that three years later the command-and-control system is still firmly entrenched. They forget that it took decades to create the extensive regulatory framework, and even if the EPA wanted to jettison the law in favor of a new, more flexible system, it is not empowered to do so.

So what's the answer? Patience.

Patience is the key as regulators, industry leaders, and ENGOs carve out a path to the new world order. It will take years, probably decades, before that new world will be ready, but when it is, this author is convinced that ISO 14001 will be a part of it. Whether that ISO 14001 role will translate into regulatory relief or merely a better system it is hard to predict, but there are encouraging signs that at the very least it will mean an enhanced relationship between the main actors in this drama.

The U.S. TAG to TC 207

One encouraging sign can be found in the inner workings of the U.S. Technical Advisory Group (TAG) to ISO Technical Committee 207 (TC 207), which is responsible for the ISO 14000 series of standards. As a former dues-paying member of this group, the author has observed representatives of the regulatory community, industry, and ENGOs working in concert to build a better environmental future. That's not to say that members of all three groups see eye-to-eye on issues. Sometimes the disagreements are strong, and even animated, but all three groups have a voice in the process of developing the U.S. position on ISO 14000 concerns. In fact, the group wanted to demonstrate the importance of having both industry and the EPA represented within the TAG, so in 1995 it elected a member of industry as its chair and an EPA official as its vice chair. Both the chair and vice chair have been reelected and are serving in their second terms. The TAG also has a number of members from the ENGO community.

These three groups have different motivations and approaches to the environment, but as a media observer who is detached from all three segments, the author believes these groups provide a check-and-balance system similar to the three branches of the U.S. government. Sure, there's friction, but its outcome is strength and viability.

TAG Chair Joseph Cascio said, "Regulatory flexibility is not going to happen the way people think it is going to happen. The EPA does not have the discretion to do so, because it is bound like everybody else to follow the law. It doesn't have the discretion to twist the laws or to soften the laws — it has got to do what it has got to do. But what is going to happen is that ISO 14001 changes the relationship between the regulated and the regulator."[1]

Cascio described the current system as a cat-and-mouse game. The regulators are chasing the mouse, and the mouse is constantly running and trying to figure out what it is going to do next. But if a regulated party puts an environmental management system (EMS) in place, it can change that relationship, putting itself on equal footing with the regulators. "All of a sudden, they are not a mouse anymore that has to scurry around and run away from a cat," said Cascio, who worked at IBM before becoming an ISO 14000 consultant. "They've taken charge of the situation. They can go to the EPA and say, 'Okay, EPA, you're a cat and I'm a cat now. I've taken charge of this; let's discuss this. And let's come up with a new relationship because we're doing a good job.' "

In fact, Cascio said that one of his clients has experienced this new relationship with its state regulators. This client was having trouble remaining in compliance and was constantly scrambling to figure out how to fix things to stay out of trouble. The state regulator had given the client six months to fix some of its problems. Then, the client implemented an environmental management system (EMS) and approached the regulator, saying that "we know we have these problems. We know we're going to fix them, and this is our schedule." The regulator responded by allowing the client the two-year schedule it requested. Cascio said the state agency wanted to know these people were in charge and that they were going to take care of their problems, and then the whole relationship changed.

"Now is that regulatory relief? Well, in my mind, that is regulatory relief. But it is regulatory relief that comes from the organization taking responsibility and taking charge, and essentially achieving a new relationship with the regulator. It is not regulatory relief that the regulators are changing the laws or modifying laws in any way, but it changes the whole relationship. And that is even more important than the traditional concept of regulatory relief, which is that you are not going to get inspected as often. ... Frankly that is the old concept of regulatory relief, which is kind of ridiculous because it is not going to happen anyway. Whereas this new thing is going to happen and is happening already. And that's what you want. You want to foster an adult-to-adult relationship. You want to foster a situation where people have respect for each other and they can work together rather than chasing each other around the block all the time, which is what they did in the old world."

Because of political pressures, the EPA is never going to be in a position to say outright that a company with an ISO 14001 registration is going to receive some regulatory advantage. Although ISO 14001 companies' relationship to EPA will change, that change will never be written on paper or acknowledged, Cascio said.

"At some future point in time, the EPA may move toward what's called performance-based regulations," he said. "Where companies may be held to levels of performance and how they do it is totally up to them, and maybe as part of that system they may need to have an environmental management system to do that, and maybe 14000 would be a part of that. But even in that case, the EPA would be looking at the performance achieved and not just the fact that it is a 14001 system. In other words, performance would be the ultimate test anyway."

But even an evolutionary move toward a performance-based system will require new statutory law enacted by Congress. "Unfortunately, in the United States the experience has been the most contentious on environment of any country. And so, unfortunately, we now have established interests in the nongovernmental, governmental, and industry," Cascio added. "We have the environmentalists, the regulators, and then we have all the lobbyists and the lawyers and the industry people who are specialized in this area, and you have all these huge numbers of people — there are tens of thousands of people who are making their living out of this confrontation. This has become a system of people fighting each other. There are thousands of lobbyists in Washington working on environmental issues. Well, if you do away with this confrontational approach and you come up with some kind of more cooperative approach, most of them are going to lose their jobs. This is big time. All the people in industry who are specialists on compliance, that's how they make their living. They understand all the nuances of the law, so they can keep the company out of trouble with the law. So you have all these interests, the environmentalists, and the 18,000 people who work for the EPA, and all the other thousands of people who work for the state government bodies. These people are all making their living out of a confrontational approach. So it's like Social Security: once you put a system in place, people depend on it and you can't get rid of it."

Other Consultants and Specialists

Marilyn R. Block, president of MRB Associates in Potomac, Maryland, said she hasn't seen any evidence of regulatory relief in the traditional sense. Some people who work in regulatory agencies might discuss what they

are doing or what is on the drawing board that might be happening in
five years, but "even for something just as simple as getting a permit, I
honestly have not seen one example where having a certificate made a
difference."[2]

Block added, "I see regulatory relief all the time on lists of benefits,
and I would like to meet a company that has actually gotten some kind
of regulatory relief. I think that there was a belief early on that by
implementing an EMS, EPA and the state departments of environment
would look kindly upon that. EPA came out with its statement saying that
they weren't going to endorse 14001. And in conjunction with that, they
modified their self-audit policy which used to provide the reduction or
elimination of the gravity-based penalty, and they got rid of that. So
identifying any regulatory compliance issues through a 14001 system does
not even result in any reduction in fines now. So, I see no evidence of
regulatory relief at this point. I think over time some states may implement
something, but I don't think that's close."

The EPA statement, released in March 1998, says that EMSs have "the
potential to improve an organization's environmental performance and
compliance." (See Appendix B for the full statement.) The EPA encourages
the use of EMSs, but does not endorse ISO 14001. The statement also
says the EPA will be working with the states on pilot projects to determine
the utility of EMSs, including those based on ISO 14001.

"I have been pleased that the EPA has been participating, putting
money into pilot programs and attempting to influence the process," said
Wayne Tusa, president of Environmental Risk and Loss Control in New
York City. "I like that because I think it makes the agency more open-
minded from both an environmental and business perspective. There are
a lot of problems with command-and-control — the biggest one being
that the system provides only financial disincentives, not financial incentives. While real significant environmental benefits have resulted from this
kind of approach, there have been a lot of inequities; it's been enormously
expensive; it's been only somewhat successful in reducing environmental
impacts and protecting public health, and now we're dealing with much
more complex issues on less obvious environmental hazards. It's much
more difficult for a command-and-control system to require minimization
of those kinds of impacts as opposed to an incentive-based system where
the system makes it worth your while to manage those same impacts."[3]

Tusa said the traditional idea of reduced command-and-control regulatory requirements in exchange for certification is not going to happen.
"Command-and-control has been useful, necessary, and it's not going
away. The environmental community and the political community would
not stand by and see the body of environmental law dismantled," he said.

Tusa said some minor benefits such as reduced monitoring might come out of this process, but he doesn't see direct regulatory relief as a major driver for ISO 14001.

"So, I sort of see the classic take on regulatory relief as somewhat of a false god — at least for now. I just don't see us throwing away command-and-control. There's too much of an investment in every sector of society, and it would be a political impossibility to convince lawmakers that eliminating command-and-control made sense. However, there can be very real indirect regulatory benefit to those organizations that implement quality environmental management systems, share that information with regulators, and, as a consequence, develop improved working relationships with those same regulators."

Anton Camarota, president of AESIR International in Annapolis, Maryland, agreed with Tusa, adding that the current U.S. regulatory structure is so antagonistic that relief will take a long time and may never happen. "Regulatory relief means you are not subject to the same regulations," he said. "I don't see the EPA doing that at all."[4]

Amy E. Schaffer, senior director of environmental program coordination at the American Forest & Paper Association (AF&PA), said regulatory relief is a future possibility, but she becomes frustrated when people make assumptions about it as a reality. Many true believers assume ISO 14001 implementation will enable state regulators to loosen their monitoring activities, but Schaffer said that "we don't know whether companies implementing 14001 really do achieve better environmental performance, and until we get that data the Multi-State Working Group is collecting, we should not be making assumptions that changing the paradigm is the right thing to do."[5]

The Multi-State Working Group on Environmental Management Systems (MSWG) and the EPA are sponsoring a national database at the University of North Carolina – Chapel Hill. Pilot projects on ISO 14001 will be capturing performance information that will be put into the national database. Some MSWG members admitted to Schaffer that they are getting pressure from their politicians to change the paradigm for two reasons, she said. First, they want to be perceived as doing regulatory reinvention. Second, they are looking to do more with less. Some in the states perceive that there will be a need for fewer inspectors and more streamlined permitting processes if the companies get buy-in from the environmental community as part of the EMS program, she said. That's why MSWG and the states are working so hard to increase public participation in ISO 14001, she added. "Basically, they are saying, 'We want you to do our job for us.' And you know what? That's not fair."

Regulatory relief is not a major driver, said Schaffer, who is chair of U.S. SubTAG 4 on environmental performance. She encouraged caution and taking steps to ensure the viability of ISO 14001 before making wholesale changes.

"I am not saying that eventually we're not going to find that, indeed, this is an excellent paradigm," she said. "I just don't want to do it until we know that it is, because I don't want the environmental community to come back and say, 'See, we told you so.' "

Schaffer and many other specialists made a distinction between regulatory relief and regulatory flexibility. Many of them said regulatory flexibility is a much more likely scenario and, in some instances, it is already occurring.

"I think that what we are seeing is that they are talking to each other as opposed to yelling at each other," Schaffer said. "What I mean is this: ISO 14001 provides a platform for discussion that is not an enforcement platform or not a permitting platform, and, as a result, there is a mutually agreed-upon goal of making the relationship better. And therefore, of course, it's going to be a better relationship. And I don't want to be cynical about it, because I think the concept of EMSs is an excellent concept, but I think it really is a matter of recognizing that you can have meaningful discussions with the regulators in a way that is not the command-and-control type of discussions. That's why they (the states) are feeling like ISO 14001 may lead to a better relationship."

Two consultants from First Environment in Riverdale, New Jersey, seemed a bit more upbeat about regulatory relief. Tod Delaney, the company's president, and Reeva Schiffman, the company's senior regulatory specialist, help companies implement ISO 14001. They said unofficial relief is occurring in some states. "You are not going to get any regulator to tell you that you are going to have regulatory relief," Schiffman said. "But the bottom line is you get it if you are implementing an EMS — at least in some states."[6]

Suzan L. Jackson, director of environmental services at Excel Partnership in Sandy Hook, Connecticut, also said she thought regulatory flexibility was occurring at two levels — the federal and the state. Pointing to the EPA statement as a positive development, Jackson said that environmental professionals are used to being pessimistic when it comes to the EPA. But upon close examination of the statement, Jackson said, it doesn't just say the EPA can't endorse ISO 14001 yet; what it is saying is the EPA is reasonably confident that environmental performance improvements will result from EMSs, but it needs proof before it can base regulatory relief on it. "That makes perfect, logical sense," Jackson said. "And they (regulators) are going after that proof by using the Multi-State Working

Group. So I actually see that policy statement as much more progressive than some environmental professionals take it. The MSWG is a very, very important piece in this whole issue of regulatory relief. That is, their whole purpose is to gather data to prove that the standard does yield environmental performance improvement."[7]

She continued, "It is all in the way you define regulatory relief. It is not reasonable to expect the EPA to back off performance levels, because there is tremendous public pressure to keep those up and even strengthen those. I think where EPA has some flexibility, and where business stands to gain the most, is looking at ways of achieving the intended results that are in line with business needs. And I think the greatest opportunity for businesses in terms of regulatory relief is where EPA focuses on the results."

Corporate Environmental Managers

Jack Bailey of Acushnet Rubber Company in New Bedford, Massachusetts, also has been an ISO 14001 leader, but he is uncertain what types of regulatory relief people want. He said Acushnet has no choice but to be in compliance, and ISO 14001 is one tool that helps the company do so. "I am audited frequently by the regulatory community, and if I'm not in compliance, I am in trouble. So this program helps me stay in compliance. That is one benefit. The idea is to go beyond compliance and get better than you actually have to be. That is the hallmark of the ISO 14001 program. So, I don't understand what kind of relief they are looking for.[8]

"Now in terms of permit flexibility, we've seen some innovation in the regulatory agencies," Bailey continued. If Acushnet wanted to change a process in the past, it had very rigid permit requirements; but now the company has been allowed by the state regulatory body to be more innovative in some of the programming and, as a result, it has reduced its emissions.

"So it has worked positively for both the regulators and our company. We think this is a major plus."

David Huyett of AlliedSignal Federal Manufacturing & Technologies in Kansas City, Missouri, said the DOE facility sees ISO 14001 as a compliance tool, not a compliance replacement. "Do it in order to be prepared for regulators when they show up," he said. "Don't do it to try to keep them from doing their job."[9]

The wrong reason to implement ISO 14001 is to obtain some regulatory relief, because the regulators have a job to do, and they are going to do it, he said. They may, over time, change their expectations and so forth, but the regulated community's job is to be prepared for them when they come, not to stop their visits.

The Multi-State Working Group

The MSWG is collecting data to meet an objective, and the ultimate vision is that the regulatory programs are going to change to reflect something like business management and the environment, said Robert Stephens of the California EPA, who serves as MSWG chair. The MSWG is formed around the idea that the state regulatory programs need to be updated in consideration of changes that are needed in addressing environmental problems, and environmental management systems may play a part in this transformation, he added. So, the MSWG is conducting research to explore the utility and viability of EMSs.[10]

"The whole data generation is really developing information of performance costs and people's roles in the process on EMS such that when we want to redesign our regulatory programs we'll have some hard information that says this works and this doesn't," Stephens said. "That is fundamentally what MSWG is about."

Stephens shied away from the term "regulatory relief," saying he preferred to look at the MSWG efforts as regulatory reinvention. "We are talking about regulatory improvements and innovations, learning how to do things better. The term 'regulatory relief' has got so much baggage associated with it. ... The common objective between the regulatory agencies and companies going toward ISO 14001 is to improve their stewardship to the environment. We are just figuring out better ways to do that."

Jeff Smoller, MSWG secretary who works for the Wisconsin Department of Natural Resources, said the MSWG is comprised of 44 states that are participants or observers who have joined with the private sector and public interest sector, plus academicians, to test EMSs in a way that will better inform everyone about their utility. Smoller noted that the database holds EMS information, not just ISO data.[11]

With respect to regulatory relief, Smoller said the states clearly see ISO 14001 as one component among many with respect to alternative regulatory systems. But one problem the MSWG has with ISO 14001 is the absence of a framework for reporting or communicating environmental performance. "As a consequence, one of the great strengths of ISO 14001 — its flexibility and adaptability — has become one of its greatest weaknesses. It prevents regulators and the public interest community from having as much confidence in it as they really should in terms of its potential."

Smoller said business also should be troubled by ISO's shortcomings because several sources now indicate ISO is being used as a substitute verification for legal compliance in some nations. If true, this raises questions of fairness.

"It is unfair for U.S. businesses to spend money to be in compliance and then spend more money for consultants to get ISO 14001 certified when their competition does not," Smoller said.

"In other words, across the border, we suspect that our competition is paying a consultant to perhaps falsely certify legal compliance," he said. "Without transparency, all we are told is 'trust us.' What's wrong with this picture?"

If widespread, Smoller said such practices could tip the playing field even more against U.S. workers. "Wait until the unions or Michael Moore find out," he said, "especially those with workers in transnational companies that are outsourcing through the supply chain."

However, the lack of transparency in ISO 14001 makes it especially suspect in the eyes of the environmental and regulatory communities, he said.

ISO 14001 is an insightful standard with international scope, but it is not meeting its full potential because of a lack of transparency, public reporting, and ambiguity on compliance, he emphasized. So, the states are not talking about regulatory reinvention based on ISO, but rather new innovations based on verifiable EMSs. Wisconsin is one of those states, Smoller said, adding that his state has a new experimental law that proffers regulatory relief for companies that implement an ISO-like EMS, but with public reporting and compliance components.

Smoller said perhaps regulatory reinvention programs will coalesce around the concept of a two-track system. On the first track, businesses may want to perform by the current system, and they have every right to do so. "They are regulated; it is a costly regulatory process; it is contentious; it is confrontational; it is litigious; but it is there, and it always will be there, as will the penalties and all of that goes with it." On the second track is a rapidly emerging alternative with an EMS component which has been used in some states, including Wisconsin, he said.

Smoller added, "Now when will it happen? Who knows. Where will it happen? Who knows. But my sense is the pace of reform will be uneven. Some states will move faster than others. Some companies within some states will move faster than others. And the challenge will be to track all these changes that are happening out there so those companies that want to take advantage of it can use the experiences of others, those pioneers. I don't think it is a question of 'if,' it is a question of 'when.' "

At least that is certainly the case in Smoller's state of Wisconsin, where state officials and the EPA have agreed to "allow regulatory relief and deferred civil enforcement in return for performance achieved through environmental management systems such as ISO 14001 'Plus.' "[12] The agreement, signed March 25 by Wisconsin and EPA officials, places Wisconsin in the company of progressive governments such as the Netherlands and Bavaria that are known for their environmental initiatives, Wisconsin Lieutenant Governor Scott McCallum told *International Environmental Systems Update (IESU)* in April 1999.

"We're making history in Wisconsin and the nation, going from a regulatory system to a performance-based system," McCallum told *IESU*.[13]

Wisconsin regulatory law remains intact, but flexibility may be extended to companies that demonstrate high environmental performance levels. State officials refer to the Wisconsin law as "ISO Plus" because it is based on the international standard but adds specific requirements on public participation and reporting, as well as compliance. Copies of the agreement can be found at the Wisconsin Department of Natural Resources web site: www.dnr.state.wi.us/org/caerkea/iso/ecpp/ecpp.htm.

The DEP

An MSWG member, Pennsylvania has one of the most progressive regulatory agencies in the country, and the Pennsylvania Department of Environmental Protection (DEP) has embraced ISO 14001 as a way of bringing about reform. One demonstration of this commitment is the employment of Ed Pinero, a high-profile ISO 14000 consultant, as the executive assistant to the deputy secretary of pollution prevention and compliance assistance at the DEP. The Office of Pollution Prevention and Compliance Assistance (OPPCA) was created in 1996 in response to Governor Tom Ridge's commitment to move away from an enforcement approach, Pinero said. "We still do enforcement, but now we have a real strong commitment to partnership with industry and the regulated community that includes a variety of different programs, all designed to help industry move beyond compliance toward sustainability rather than just satisfying ourselves with just compliance."[14]

He continued, "One of the real telling statistics is if you look at compliance statistics, our industry in this state is approximately in 90 percent compliance. In other words, 90 percent of our industry is actually compliant. We ask ourselves, 'Are we saying then that we feel that we are that close to being perfect in terms of environmental conditions?' The answer is no. There is a lot that can be done in terms of energy efficiency and resource conservation. We ask ourselves what we can do different, because, obviously, only getting people to compliance is not going to be far enough. That is where the whole commitment to a sustainable regulatory approach to industry comes, rather than just having enforcement."

The OPPCA developed a strategic environmental management (SEM) policy that provides guidance to the department on how to conduct business, Pinero said. One of the goals outlined in the SEM policy is zero emissions. "Using zero emissions as the philosophy of the goal of the SEM policy, we talked about several tools that can be used, which is enhanced community involvement, pollution prevention, and efficiency kind of thinking, using environmental cost accounting and environmental performance indicators to kind of see how you are doing. In all of that, we say using an environmental management system is an excellent infrastructure upon which to build all of your performance goals toward this zero emissions philosophy. That is where ISO 14001 comes in. We feel that it is an excellent mechanism upon which to build your environmental performance infrastructure. What is critical about that is being an ISO-14001 certified company in and of itself is not a goal. It is not the be-all and end-all of this process. ISO 14000, in our opinion, is one tool which can be used to build your system.

"Our expectation is that if you say that you are going to conform to the SEM philosophy, you will use something like the most logical choice, which is ISO 14001. It is the only internationally recognized standard out there for EMSs. But you will use an EMS to meet these performance goals."

The DEP's position statement on strategic environmental management is designed to provide a framework for the state's businesses and municipalities, according to materials on the DEP web site, www.dep.state.pa.us. The policy outlines the key elements of SEM as fourfold: (1) environmental management system, (2) pollution prevention program, (3) community involvement program, and (4) performance measures.

Implementing the DEP's philosophy of strategic environmental management is strictly voluntary, Pinero said, adding that companies that want to concern themselves exclusively with compliance are allowed to do so. But the DEP hopes its businesses will see the value of going beyond compliance.

And Pennsylvania does have some model companies that have implemented ISO 14001, such as Wilton Armetale in Mount Joy and Warner-Lambert in Lititz. Among its many proactive initiatives, the DEP has pilot projects involved in the MSWG efforts to compile the national database. Klein Plating Works in Erie was the first Pennsylvania company to join the MSWG project, and it was followed by the World Resources Company in Pottsville; PennDOT, the first transportation agency in the country to participate in the MSWG pilot project; and the Pittsburgh International Airport.[15] Pinero said the DEP's participation in the MSWG pilot represents the state's desire to work in partnership to discover information about the effectiveness of ISO 14001, and EMSs in general.[16]

On the subject of regulatory relief, Pinero said the terms used to describe it vary from state to state, making the subject awkward to discuss. "We have taken two positions on this when it comes to the subject of regulatory relief," said Pinero, formerly of EnSafe in Memphis, Tennessee. "We are not writing into regulations things like: if you are ISO 14001 certified, you do not need permit X. We can't do that. Our job is to carry out and implement law. That kind of change would have to come at the legislative level. ... We do not have a very good handle on how being ISO 14001 certified translates into improved environmental performance. Intuitively, we know it is the case; and personally, I have dealt with this in the last four years around the world. I see it happening. But it has to be more tangible before you see states going to the extreme of actually changing their entire legislative infrastructures. However, in terms of being proactive and open-minded, that is what the MSWG program is trying to do."

Through the national database, regulators can arm themselves with EMS performance data from the pilot projects to effect reform, he said. The project is slated to examine data for the next couple of years, he noted.

Pinero said that the DEP is providing technical assistance and trying to undergird its businesses toward the zero emissions goal. But in all honesty, he said, the DEP still has its enforcement arm, because some people out there couldn't care less about this and they try to get away with whatever they can. So, regardless of the outcome of the MSWG pilot project and regulatory reform, enforcement will always be a part of the system, he said. While enforcement will remain, Pinero is talking to people who are excited about the emergence of a second track in which companies that are proactive on the environment might be treated differently. "How that plays out will vary from state to state," he said. "It will vary on what the EPA ultimately does with their efforts because we obviously have to respond to the federal law."

As a consultant prior to joining the DEP, Pinero had helped several companies implement an EMS, and from his experiences, he said the clamor for regulatory relief has subsided. Companies are reaping so many other benefits of implementing an EMS and working toward sustainable technologies that "we lost that deep urgency of 'the only way I can pull this off is if you don't make me file this permit or if you stop making me do this.' We have not heard that (request) much. ... The regulatory relief is not as critical anymore. In entering into these memorandums with companies on these pilot projects, no one has asked for this break or that break. They are doing it because they see it as a performance and an internal improvement mechanism."

Maybe in a few years, when ISO 14001 is more mature, state regulatory agencies can think about relief, but they don't have the flexibility to do it without more concrete proof, he said. "Even if we are convinced that this will result in improved performance, if we cannot show it, the general public will feel slighted," he said. "The department has flexibility, like how many times it inspects companies. But even before ISO that type of flexibility was exercised. Violators were visited more often than nonviolators. That is, in essence, regulatory flexibility."

The U.S. EPA

In March 1998, the U.S. Environmental Protection Agency (EPA) published its position statement on ISO 14000, offering some hope while giving others pause. Some believed the statement was weak, while others characterized it as reasonable and even progressive. But one thing the statement undoubtedly accomplished was to put ISO 14000 into the public policy arena. Previously, EPA members had participated in the U.S. TAG and some had made various statements, but this position statement marked an official agency opinion that ISO 14000 should be elevated as a public policy issue — an issue that should be explored and examined before any wholesale changes could result.

But even before EPA published the statement, the agency was working on a number of voluntary initiatives designed to enhance regulatory reinvention. Several of these programs, such as Project XL or Energy Star, are part of the EPA's overall Partners for Environment concept. The EPA collaborates with more than 8000 organizations through the Partners for Environment programs, according to an EPA web site: www.epa.gov/reinvent. Materials from the web site indicate that Partners for the Environment companies racked up impressive results in 1997. These companies:

- Reduced air pollution by preventing 79 million metric tons of carbon dioxide emissions
- Saved nearly 6 million gallons of clean water
- Stopped 7.6 million tons of solid waste from entering landfills

- Saved 1020 trillion British Thermal Units (BTUs), or enough energy to light 56 million homes for a year
- Saved $1.6 billion collectively

Ted Cochin, who has written ISO 14000 articles and is working in the EPA Office of Reinvention, works with the national pilot program called "Project XL," which stands for eXellence and Leadership. XL is designed to test innovative ways of achieving better and more-cost-effective public health and environmental protection. Through site-specific agreements with project sponsors, EPA is gathering data and project experience that will help the agency redesign current approaches to public health and environmental protection. Under Project XL sponsors — private facilities, multiple facilities, industry sectors, federal facilities, communities, and states — can implement innovative strategies that produce superior environmental performance through pollution prevention, greater accountability to stakeholders, cost savings, paperwork reduction, or other benefits to sponsors. Cochin said when potential project sponsors have a certain issue with a policy or regulation that they think is hampering their ability to conduct business in the way they want to, or have a new approach to try out, they can come to EPA with their concerns. "EPA will ask the sponsor to write up a project proposal that includes the flexibility, and then EPA would require that the project proposal will produce superior environmental performance. A lot of potential sponsors have come up with project ideas that include the development and implementation of an EMS, or a similar type of a management system that incorporates innovative approaches such as design for the environment, total cost accounting, or industrial ecology. Sponsors are encouraged to come up with their own innovative approaches to demonstrate that their project will produce superior environmental performance, involve all relevant stakeholder groups, and go beyond compliance. ... I would say that to satisfy the XL criteria, a sponsor will have to have some type of EMS framework in place. In most cases, the systems that they would have in place will exceed the environmental performance requirements of most traditional EMSs."[17]

Cochin emphasized that the regulatory flexibility is extended because the sponsors must meet XL criteria producing:

- Superior environmental results;
- Benefits such as cost savings and paperwork reduction;
- Stakeholder involvement and support;
- Innovation and pollution prevention;
- Transferable data;

- Feasibility that the project will work at the given facility;
- Accountability through monitoring, reporting, and evaluation; and
- Avoidance of shifting risk burden.

Cochin, who worked with Jack Bailey at Acushnet Rubber Company before going to the EPA, said command-and-control will never be done away with because the country needs the regulations to some extent. "In addition to the obvious functions of stopping pollution, they make it more expensive to use certain toxic or hazardous chemicals and materials, and promote pollution prevention and source reduction in many instances. There is definitely a need there," Cochin said. "I think we also need to have a shift toward more of a voluntary way of looking at things for those companies that are good performers and are out there really trying. I do not think anyone wants to give away the whole system, but I think that for those companies with excellent compliance histories, we want to give incentives to go beyond compliance. The disincentives are regulations, but you should also have incentives such as public recognition, or some type of flexibility in policies or regulations that would encourage companies to concentrate on the public health and environmental risks that their companies are producing. Many of these risks may not be addressed by current regulations."

Cochin added, "I think the EPA is going to continue experimenting in the area of regulatory and policy flexibility. We are currently working to expand this approach to work with trade associations with various industrial sectors, in which new rules will come out in a particular sector based on XL. Many of the lessons learned through experimentation will be showing up in future rules and policies at the federal and state levels. Potential project sponsors that I talk to have certain issues that go against common sense; a lot of these issues are related to the way that states or the EPA conduct their business where things just don't make any sense from the standpoint of efficiency or environmental protection. I work primarily with industrial facilities in various manufacturing sectors. The corporate leaders and EHS folks at these companies want to try out something new, and we say, 'Sure,' as long as it meets our criteria. We are granting that flexibility on a case-by-case basis, and I see it expanding further so that we can learn and evolve."

In addition to the EPA's plethora of Partners for Environment programs, the agency has initiated another pilot to test the viability of ISO 14001 for the public sector. The EPA Offices of Wastewater Management and Compliance have worked on a two-year project usually referred to as the "Municipalities Initiative," even though not all participants are municipalities. The participants include seven municipalities, one county, and one state prison system that are implementing an ISO 14001 EMS, but each participant has the freedom to decide whether to pursue certification to the standard. The participants are:

- Londonderry, New Hampshire
- Lowell, Massachusetts
- Wayne County, Michigan
- Indianapolis, Indiana
- Massachusetts Department of Corrections
- Gaithersburg, Maryland
- Lansing Board of Water & Light in Michigan
- Scottsdale, Arizona
- New York City Transit Authority[18]

Jim Horne, EPA Office of Wastewater Management, said, "The use of voluntary environmental management systems (EMS) by organizations is rapidly increasing around the world. These systems provide a framework for organizations and communities to more effectively manage their environmental obligations, including those required to comply with applicable statutes and regulations."[19]

The EPA hired the Global Environment Technology Foundation as its consulting firm to help the municipalities implement the ISO 14001 EMS and, to date, several of the municipalities have seen real results from their ISO 14001 efforts.

Mike Toledo, deputy superintendent of operations at the Massachusetts Department of Corrections in Norfolk, said the state agency is committed to taking an active role on environmental issues, as well as enhancing its good relationship with surrounding communities. And the state department of corrections might consider expanding ISO 14001 throughout the entire system if the Norfolk facility, which is in the municipalities project, produces desirable results.

"It is our desire that through implementation of the ISO 14001 EMS, employees will realize the benefits, not only for the department and the commonwealth, but in their own lives as well as those of their family and friends," Toledo said. "Having an effective environmental management system is a win-win situation. Further, an effective EMS not only impacts our environment but also improves employee safety and awareness."[20]

Toledo said the biggest challenge the facility faced was time. All of the people involved in the project have other full-time duties and responsibilities, and much of the work completed to date had been achieved during off-hours, at home, and on weekends. "We had a difficult time at first but once momentum began, it became noticeably easier. Also, unexpected changes in our original core team came all at once. That forced us to retrain a new group of people that we knew would be self-motivated, composed of a sampling of all areas within the facility as well as having knowledge of all functions and operating systems for each of the three areas within our selected fence line. Lastly, core team members had to have or have access to all applicable laws and regulations that affected our fence-line facilities. We are fortunate to have people who bought into the program from the start and have remained dedicated throughout. That, in itself, is a key element to the success of accepting and completing such a task."

He continued, "It would be difficult to implement an effective EMS and not realize some degree of cost savings. The facilities within our fence line are very small by comparison to most companies implementing an EMS. The quantities of raw materials/products we use are minute when compared to large businesses. However, the process that implementation of ISO 14000 dictates forced us to examine not only what we use but how it is used. If there is something that could be used or done differently and would result in a cost savings, it would likely be identified through the implementation process.

"The thing that we feel will be most beneficial and will result in cost savings to our operations are the procedures that have been or are being developed that will aid in the prevention or elimination of possible spills and other accidents which may either contaminate our surrounding environment or cause injuries to our employees. Taking the necessary measures to avoid the costs associated with clean-up, disposal of contaminated waste, corrective actions, fines, and medical care as a result of such an event, while difficult to project, can be realized as a significant savings to the department. Lastly, improving our standing and image with our surrounding communities as well as the environmental community in general is, in itself, beneficial to a municipality or any facility serving the public."

Toledo said that in time the department will know how big an impact that ISO 14001 implementation will have on its operations from a business standpoint, but "at an absolute minimum, anytime you can bring a team of co-workers together for the purpose of working toward such a major undertaking as implementing an ISO 14001 EMS, the benefits are substantial and rewarding."

Amy McClure, project manager for the city of Indianapolis, Indiana, said the city has focused on its operations garages for its pilot program, and is considering expanding it. The operations garages have a history of being reactive to problems, and city officials hoped participation in the municipalities project would make them more proactive. "We sat down with our operations people. We developed an implementation team that consisted of people from the operations division, legal, and finance. We asked them their opinion of what needs to be done. We went through and broke down every activity that is performed within our operations garages. Out of those activities, we had them rank the ones they thought needed to be addressed most, or the quickest or most environmentally threatening. There was a long list, and we narrowed it down to five, and from those five we chose to work on one in particular that we feel really needs to be addressed, and that is our drum management issue."[21]

She said she anticipates saving money through drum management. The Indianapolis operations garages have accumulation of a large number of drums — some of which did not even originate from the garages. People were dumping the drums on city property, and the drums are very expensive to discard. The operations garages have begun to control the number of drums generated, raising awareness within the community, and they intend to measure the results by the percentage of reduction in drums used.

Pointing to the bulk delivery and drum disposal, McClure said talking about the issue as a business problem, rather than an environmental issue, helped her sell the idea. McClure said that talking about the carelessness of opening too many drums as an environmental problem will not register with most employees, but when she tells them that their lives are going to be easier if the city implements a new system, then they buy into the new way of doing things.

"I think there is definitely a place for environmental management within municipalities because they deal with a lot of environmental issues," McClure said. "... ISO is a good background for looking at your different aspects and trying to address them. I do not know if I am 100 percent sold on the documentation and all of the things that go along with it because, within a municipality, it is very difficult to keep track of that documentation through the change in administrations that happens so frequently. One administration could come in and say, 'What is this program? You are not doing it anymore.' Then it means nothing. If you have an EMS in place, those are business practices, and the union people who are practicing those (procedures) do not change. That personnel does not change. They are there a lot longer than an administration."

Elizabeth Todd, division supervisor for solid waste and recycling for the town of Londonderry, New Hampshire, said the town decided to participate in the Municipalities Initiative because it was not proud of its environmental past. Londonderry has three Superfund sites. (Superfund is a program designed to clean up the country's hazardous waste sites.)

"Basically, we learned our lesson, and we want to be conscious about our impact on the environment," Todd said. She noted that Londonderry also had more than the average number of commuters, and it wanted to make sure that the town minimizes its impact on the environment.[22]

Londonderry is focusing its ISO 14001 initiative on the public works department, which has four divisions: solid waste, sewer, engineering, and highway. "We chose those because we felt that those had the most significant impact on the environment."

Londonderry has initiated several programs as a result of its ISO 14001 activities. For example, the highway garage focused on better materials management to lower waste disposal costs by using nontoxic materials whenever possible. Londonderry's highway garage also decided not to buy any more disposable rags, opting to buy reusable ones. "That will certainly save us money, but I do not have a specific dollar figure (yet)." Also, lowering trash quantities for solid waste will lower disposal costs, currently charged by the ton.

The Londonderry Town Council bought into the ISO 14001 project because of the potential cost savings, she said, adding that it costs millions of dollars to clean up the town's landfill. "Cost was one of our focuses as well as the fact that the town had grown so much, and we wanted to preserve some of the character of the town, which includes the orchards that are a historical part of Londonderry."

One of the biggest benefits to date has been improved communications among the four divisions, she said. "We all seem to be really busy, and we never seem to communicate. It has been a really good way to highlight problems and issues that have not been brought up before. It has been a really good way to get communication between the different divisions. I would say that was a really good benefit of the program."

The Municipalities Initiative is one of many pilot projects the U.S. EPA has launched in an attempt to capture implementation information. But in other parts of the world, regulatory flexibility and ISO 14001 go hand-in-hand. Other regions of the globe like China, Japan, and Bavaria have embraced ISO 14001 as a way to handle their industries' impact on the environment. The home of one-fifth of the world's population, China announced in April 1997 that it would adopt the voluntary series of standards as state policy.[23] Japan leads the world in ISO 14001 certifications, while the Bavarian government has developed an alternative "regulatory substitution" system based on EMSs.[24]

The Netherlands

Perhaps one of the best examples of regulatory relief across the globe can be found in the Netherlands. The Netherlands' Central Ministry of Environment has a model of regulatory relief based on ISO 14001 certification that is being tested in a variety of pilot projects.[25] Dick Hortensius, a senior environmental standardization consultant at the Netherlands Normalisantie Institute (NNI), said this model has resulted in an increase in ISO 14001 certifications. According to the latest statistics, the Netherlands had more than 300 certifications to the EMS standard.[26]

The new model outlines a process in which companies are issued global environmental licenses that focus more on EMS objectives than the technical aspects of environmental management. Companies are given more freedom on how to meet those objectives, but an enforcement element remains.[27]

"ISO 14001 has been very well accepted in the Netherlands," Hortensius said. "At a seminar on ISO 14000 organized by NNI in 1996, the Dutch minister for environment said that the publication of ISO 14001 was to be considered an important milestone, although the current version of ISO 14001 should not be seen as the endpoint; future EMSs should be more focused on product-related environmental aspects. At the same seminar, the chairman of the Dutch Federation of Employers also stated that the ISO 14000 series of standards is a key issue for Dutch industry. Implementation of ISO 14000 means being up-to-date and will facilitate communication about environmental issues with suppliers and customers. This positive attitude has not changed. Government stimulates ISO 14001 implementation and provides incentives such as regulatory relief (environmental licensing and enforcement). All interested parties (government, industry, ENGOs, labor organizations) cooperate in the harmonized Dutch certification system."

Hortensius continued, "Potential regulatory relief is an important incentive, especially for larger companies. Implementation of ISO 14001 provides the possibility to get a so-called 'license on main issues' or 'outline license.' This means, in essence, that requirements in the license are specifying objectives (environmental performance levels) and not the technical means to achieve those objectives. The ISO 14001 system (preferably certified) should provide confidence that the company can manage its environmental aspects in a sound way, and that it will be able to achieve the specified environmental performance levels."

He added, "Regulatory relief is important because it can be a win-win situation. Government does not have to bother about all sorts of technical details and can focus on what is really important for society: the level of environmental performance of companies. And companies get more free-dom in managing their business. On a more general level, a more sustainable society can only be achieved with conscious, self-responsible, and proactive industry. ISO 14000 provides industry with essential tools to play that role, and government should reward companies that show good willingness and behavior. Not all environmental issues can be legally regulated, government needs self-responsible companies that manage their own environmental aspects."

Regardless of the location on the globe, the regulators and the regulated should work together to enhance their relationships. And perhaps for some, ISO 14001 can be a significant key to unlocking the tangled web of regulations that seemingly have imprisoned corporations and regulatory agencies in an adversarial game of cat and mouse.

Notes

1. Cascio, J., personal interview, November 6, 1998.
2. Block, M. R., telephone interview, October 19, 1998.
3. Tusa, W., telephone interview, September 15, 1998.
4. Camarota, A. G., telephone interview, November 5, 1998.
5. Schaffer, A. E., telephone interview, November 24, 1998.
6. Delaney, T., and Schiffman, R., telephone interview, January 29, 1999.
7. Jackson, S. L., telephone interview, November 18, 1998.
8. Bailey, J., telephone interview, November 5, 1998.
9. Huyett, D., telephone interview, November 4, 1998.
10. Stephens, R., telephone interview, January 14, 1999.
11. Smoller, J., telephone interview, January 11, 1999.
12. State of Wisconsin, U.S. EPA Strike Deal for Regulatory Relief: Agreement Calls for EMS Performance Results in Exchange, *International Environmental Systems Update,* 4(6), 1999.
13. Ibid.
14. Pinero, E., telephone interview, January 13, 1999.
15. The Pennsylvania Department of Environmental Protection's web site: www.dep.state.pa.us, 1999.
16. Pinero, telephone interview.
17. Cochin, T., telephone interview, February 3, 1999.
18. Implementing ISO 14001 Environmental Management Systems at the Municipal Level, Global Environment & Technology Foundation web site, globeNet, 1998.
19. Ibid.
20. Toledo, M., written question-and-answer interview, February 16, 1999.
21. McClure, A., telephone interview, January 7, 1999.
22. Todd, E., telephone interview, January 8, 1999.

23. China Adopts 14000 as State Policy, *International Environmental Systems Update*, 4(1), 1987.

24. Wyman, M., and Feldman, I., EMS and 'Regulatory Substitution' in Bavaria: New Approach Streamlines Alternate Regulatory System, *International Environmental Systems Update*, 9(17), 1998.

25. St. Ours, D., Dutch Government Issues Environmental Licenses: Regulatory Relief Seen as Incentive for ISO 14001 Certification, *International Environmental Systems Update*, 4(18), 1998.

26. Hortensius, D., online interview via e-mail, November 11, 1998.

27. St. Ours, *IESU*, p. 18.

Chapter 7

Insurance and Other Financial Breaks

"When ISO 14001 was first released, the only thing that exceeded the promise of regulatory relief was the promise of insurance benefits," said Jeff Smoller, a key leader within the Multi-State Working Group on Environmental Management Systems. "And I think that both have proved elusive. And so I think right now you have ISO 14001, which is kind of in a critical part of its life cycle, where companies and others are basically saying, 'Where's the beef? or Where's the relief? Where's the rate relief?' I think that is coming. And the answer for those who are asking (these questions) is to be patient."[1]

Many within ISO 14000 circles had long awaited the specification standard, hoping that companies' commitment to implementing ISO 14001 would translate into insurance and other financial breaks from lending institutions. But for the most part, lenders and insurers remain hesitant to give a company an insurance break based solely on ISO 14001. They have said that development in this area will be slow until the standard is revised to reflect a greater commitment to compliance, and to provide some kind of metrics or baseline to measure companies' environmental performance against one another.

Others have tried to draw conclusions about environmental performance and financial performance — does having an EMS translate into higher stock prices? As noted in previous chapters, an EMS can translate into a healthier bottom line, and it would seem logical that a better bottom line means better stock prices or corporate value for shareholders. But while studies seem to support this obvious logic, it is difficult to prove a direct cause and effect between an EMS and higher stock prices. It's also true that it is hard to isolate the EMS as the sole reason for the better stock prices, because most companies with an aggressive, proactive EMS have a forward-thinking management team that has most likely implemented other corporate improvements. While it is fair to say that an EMS may contribute to higher stock prices, it seems virtually impossible to pinpoint it as the sole cause.

The Insurance Angle

Mark Zimmerman, assistant vice president for ECS Risk Control, Inc., whose sister company ECS Underwriting is an underwriting manager for environmental pollution insurance, said there has been some slight movement on the insurance front related to ISO 14000 — but it is limited to only a couple of insurance companies. Zimmerman said his company has issued statements supporting the ISO 14000 efforts, but from a practical standpoint, the standard has holes in it. His company also supports any attempts to build an index line against which insurance underwriters can measure the corporation's commitment to good, solid environmental practices.[2]

"In many respects, ISO 14001 is a great idea in that it provides a global instrument that is common everywhere, and which I think is needed," Zimmerman said. "But it doesn't do enough, in my opinion, to represent the players, the people who actually get the certificate, and where they stand against each other and across dissimilar industries as well."

Addressing the main holes he perceived in the standard, Zimmerman would like to be able to analyze how the environmental performance of two ISO 14001-certified companies match up, because if he is going to offer breaks, he needs to be able to rate companies against each other. "We need to be able to assign premiums based on the risk that each of those companies possesses, not on what that business class presents. To do it profitably, we need to know what ABC Tank does down the road and XYZ Tank does up the road. Both of them have the certification, but that does not tell me enough from the outside as a loss control professional or as an underwriter. We need to know each company's operational profiles. That is where we have to come in and audit them, or we have to gain access to the ISO 14001 audit.

"Give me some metrics and give me an index line," he said to standards writers who will revise ISO 14001. "Publish a company with a number and tell me that the company is a one, two, three, four, or five. ... Our company is supportive of any attempt to provide standards that gauge companies' performance. It is important for us and is in our best interest to do so. We (previously) have lobbied heavily for that in the state and federal government to provide the same standards for environmental consulting companies." (But he noted the company had not been active in this area for some time.)

ECS Risk Control audits companies to determine, based on the way they operate and make decisions, whether they have a higher or lower risk of having a claim in the future, he said. In weighing the potential risk, Zimmerman considers how a company thinks about the environment and whether it has an environmental management system as part of the overall evaluation.

"Everyone is going to have a claim," Zimmerman said. "No matter how good you are, you are going to stub your toe. We are not going to penalize you for that. What we are interested in is how adaptive is a company in responding to that situation? Is the company quick to address the problem right away? Or does it try to deny it? Is the company going to deny it and let it get bigger and bigger? Or is it going to respond immediately? We ask questions to try to elicit that type of information. ... So, we need to consider the nature of business that that company is doing. An EMS is one element of that. It is a solid and fundamental element, but it is one element of the exposure profile."

Zimmerman said that if a company has an ISO 14001 certificate, he would see that as a positive factor, but he needs metrics in place that give him a quantifiable relationship. "That way we can adjust your premium to reflect your lowered risk profile."

But he said a few insurance companies are looking at insurance adjustments based solely on environmental management systems.

The John Roberts Company

In fact, the 80th largest commercial printer in the United States got an unexpected surprise from its insurance carrier because of its environmental management and safety loss control system.

Insurance companies are in business for one reason: to make money. So, it is hard to imagine why any insurance carrier would give away free insurance coverage — particularly to cover a risk that most insurers will not touch. But that's exactly the good fortune that befell The John Roberts Company in Minneapolis, Minnesota.

Jeffrey R. Adrian, environmental director at The John Roberts Company, said the company was fielding bids from prospective insurance carriers for all of its coverage, and one insurance carrier secured the business by making a unique and shrewd offer. The carrier came back with the best rates and offered to give The John Roberts Company pollution spill coverage at no cost. The reason? The printer had an aggressive, strong environmental management system and safety loss control (EMS/SLC) program. To secure the business, Atlantic Mutual told John Roberts Company, "We're going to give you something that you practically cannot buy at any price," Adrian said. "That is, we're going to give you pollution spill coverage at no cost to you."[3]

While it was an unusual move, Adrian said it was a smart one, because Atlantic Mutual's actuary people saw that the company's EMS/SLC kept risk to a minimum, and it helped them secure the business. "Clearly, this is outside-the-box thinking because now we are viewing an EMS and loss control program for the first time as an asset instead of always regarding this sort of thing, anything environmental, on the liability side of the ledger. Now it has cash value. And that is new thinking — whether that will spread to other companies, I don't know."

Adrian said the free coverage is worth $10,000 a year. "It's a little thing, but show me someone else who's got it. No one else does. And if we had an accident, we've got several million dollars worth of coverage. That's pretty cool. It's shrewd marketing on their part."

With nearly 400 employees and $65 million in sales, the printing company pursued an EMS, although not ISO 14001, for several reasons:

- To reduce exposure to liability;
- To increase management efficiency;
- To seize the opportunity to eliminate duplicative efforts;
- To improve employee relations;
- To improve community relations; and
- To take advantage of opportunities for partnering with the community, regulatory agencies, and public interest groups.[4]

"All of these things have a link to what I call bottom-line savings," Adrian said. "Sometimes they are hard to measure directly, but they are there."

The John Roberts Company looks at the environment in a larger context that includes energy consumption, and it has slashed its natural gas usage by one-third through Maximum Achievable Control Technology (MACT). The company's expenditure for natural gas usage dropped from more than $70,000 a year to close to $30,000.

The company also saves $23,000 annually through a program in which the printer recycles its own solvent back to the Minneapolis facility. The solvents are used to clean the printing presses and, previously, John Roberts spent about $28,000 to $30,000 a year in hazardous waste disposal of the solvents. Through a partnership with the original supplier and what would be the disposal site, John Roberts sends the solvent to that licensed treatment and storage disposal facility and, instead of fuel blending it for disposal, it is distilled. The distillate, which is now a by-product, is shipped back to the original vendor where it is processed and shipped back to John Roberts.

Adrian said recycling projects could be accomplished without an EMS, but an EMS helps companies manage them. For example, he said one of the biggest examples of revenue back to the company for a printer can be found in capturing the trim waste. Printers can recover the trim waste and have it recycled into paper at a paper mill. Looking at September 1998 figures, Adrian said The John Roberts Company recouped $32,159 that month in recycled trim waste. "Multiply that out $32,000 times 12 months and you are looking at $384,000 a year," he said. "That's some serious money. That's just from paper.

"Can you do these things without an EMS? Yeah, but you increase your likelihood of finding opportunities if you have an EMS. The art comes after you pick the low-hanging fruit, and you are done and you say to yourself, 'Well, now what do you do to go after even greater things?' That's where your EMS and safety loss control program can really help."

John Roberts Company also invested in new technology that reduces the use of solvents. The company spent $17,500 on a dry ice mini blaster, which works similar to a sand blaster only without using sand, to clean the printing presses. Previously, the company had to use harsh solvents that evaporate quickly and put volatile organic compounds (VOCs) in the air. But the new technology that blasts gummy substances off the intricate parts of the presses is faster, cleaner, and avoids exposure to chemicals for employees and the environment. "The only protective steps we have to take is hearing protection, because it tends to be loud," he added.

To have a successful EMS/SLC program, a company has to manage up as well as down. Adrian has developed a set of starter questions that he asks every month to help keep the EMS/SLC program on track (Figure 7.1). "Keep in mind that the other parties in this situation within a corporation really don't care about the environment, per se. I mean they do, but they don't. If you go and talk the wrong language, you are not going to get through to them."

Referring to the company's new air emissions controls, Adrian continued, "Our air emissions control burns at 1300 degrees Fahrenheit. So what?

Figure 7.1

Sample Starter Questions

These are good questions that should be asked and answered every month as a part of your Environmental Management System & Safety Loss Control Plan. This review process serves nicely as the Checking & Corrective Action part of the EMS/SLC. This is also about managing up as well as down.

- Where do we stand with compliance issues at this time? Do we currently have any noncompliance issues? What are they? What reports and plans will need to be filed say, within the next one or two months?

- What environmental projects do we have coming up that will affect the budget in a significant way?

- What is the status of various legislative actions that will affect how the company will operate over the next year, and possibly future years? How are we coming with our legislative outreach efforts?

- What major new agency rulemaking will affect the company operations in the future? What kind of an impact will they make on our ability to grow from your perspective?

- How is the company progressing towards its pollution prevention goals?

- What special projects are you currently working on, and what is the status of those projects?

- What are your current areas of concern? Where are you having the greatest difficulty? How can I help you?

- Are we compensating you appropriately for your contribution to the company (ask once every two months)?

Source: From Jeffrey R. Adrian, environmental director, The John Roberts Company. With permission.

Figure 7.1

Do you think my production manager cares? What he cares about are production-related things. He cares that I don't have to do big interruptive type things, that the equipment is reliable, that he doesn't have a lot of shutdowns. That's what he cares about — that's p-talk or production talk. If I talk to him about environmental benefits, I'm not going to communicate with him. Do you think my CFO cares? He doesn't care that it burns at 1300 degrees, but he does care that we use one-third of the natural gas that we used to. That's dollars. ... My point here is that all of these people suffer from EADD — Executive Attention Deficient Disorder. You have about three minutes, and to make that time effective, you better figure out how to talk the other guys' language. So, you change environmental talk to business talk. Unless I can relate things down to dollars and cents, I've got a hard time. That's just the way business works. And frankly, I think that's the right way to do things. The worst reason to do something in this area is because the regulations say so. If I can't give you a better reason than that, you should fire me. I'm not doing my job. You'll have greater staying power if you do it for your bottom line than if you do it just to meet regulations."

Adrian said the company's EMS did not start out as an EMS, but rather as a loss control program. In pursuing an SLC, the company soon discovered a tremendous potential for a bottom-line payoff in having an EMS as well, so it worked on integrating both EMS and SLC into one program. "John Roberts Company eventually ended up mentoring their EMS to other companies," he said. "In 1995, John Roberts Company was one of 12 companies selected to participate in the EPA's Environmental Leadership Pilot Program. Our project during 1995–1996 would be to mentor to a group of small printers that range in size from 18 to 62 employees."[5]

Addressing ISO 14001, Adrian said, "ISO 14001 is a great model. It is something to look at. There's certainly a lot that you can take from it. What is the question mark at this point is the marketing capacity: is it market-driven enough to actually more forward? If you are definitely marketing overseas and you need to have a program of some sort that is harmonized with the programs in Europe, ISO 14001 is probably a pretty good bet. If that is not the case, and I would argue at least at this time it doesn't appear to be the case for a large number of companies, then you are faced with another question. And the other question is: is there a strong basis for looking at an environmental management system, whether it's ISO 14001? Why wait until you have to do ISO 14001?"[6]

In the area of financing, Adrian pointed out an issue on the tax front. For example, if John Roberts Company buys a new printing press, it does not have to pay a state sales tax. But if it buys $500,000 worth of pollution prevention or control equipment, the company does have to pay sales tax. "Now what is the message we are sending," he said. "Do we mean to send that message? Is that really what we want to do as a society?"

A Better Bond Rating

The town of Londonderry, New Hampshire, is participating in the U.S. Environmental Protection Agency's municipalities project, and it received a favorable bond rating, probably in part because of its ISO 14001 efforts. Elizabeth Todd, division supervisor for solid waste and recycling for the Town of Londonderry, said the town's bond rating went from an A to an Aa-3 rating, improving about one point.[7]

Although no one directly expressed to Todd that ISO 14001 had anything to do with the new bond rating, it was among the information submitted and considered. "When our bond rating was approved, they did not say directly that it was a result of the ISO program, but I think that it did have an impact on their decision on the whole," she said.

Looking for a Direct Link

There's a great deal of talk, speculation, and hope that as ISO 14001 matures, it will translate into financial benefits — anything from enhanced stock prices to the increased ability to secure business loans. But when it comes to concrete direct evidence that ISO 14001 has enhanced a company's ability to secure bank loans or raised the stock value, no one seems to have any — at least not the kind set in stone.

"I am actually unaware of anything concrete on the finance side that is tying it specifically to ISO 14000," said Ed Weiler, an economist with the U.S. EPA, who quickly added that doesn't mean "somebody, somewhere is not doing something along those lines." But he is confident such activities would not be mainstream.[8]

Pointing back to a 1997 roundtable discussion in Washington on the subject, Weiler said that industry representatives had many questions about what ISO 14001 certification meant. "I just heard nothing that would lend itself to the notion that the ISO certification would somehow translate into more favorable finance terms," Weiler said. Some saw ISO 14001 certification as a favorable indication of the "forward lookingness" of management, but that is a gigantic leap from a drive toward concrete, favorable loan terms, he added.

Another item that came out of that meeting, he said, was the reality that ISO 14001 alone may be too narrow a criterion to secure favorable loan rates. ISO 14001 would have to be considered among other business factors. So many people are exploring how environmental performance affects financial performance, but the problem is pinpointing a direct cause-and-effect.

For example, ICF Kaiser International, Inc. in Fairfax, Virginia, released a major study in January 1997 that indicated shareholder wealth could be boosted by up to five percent when public companies enhance their environmental practices. Exploring more than 300 public companies in the United States, the study seemed to show that reducing environmental risk could enhance stock prices. Titled, "Does Improving a Firm's Environmental Management System and Environmental Performance Result in a Higher Stock Price?," the study does not assert a direct cause and effect, but offers some help for senior managers who want to make the logical leap from environmental performance to economic performance.[9]

"We believe that sound environmental management leads to reduced risk to the firm, and that this risk reduction is valued by financial markets. ... Lower risks mean lower required returns, and therefore, lower costs for financing the activities of the firm," the authors of the study wrote.[10]

The study is available at ICF Kaiser's home page at http://www.icfkaiser.com.[11]

What about Wall Street?

Some observers speculate that Wall Street may begin to take notice of environmental performance as an economic indicator, but again, the proof that is occurring is scant at best. In July 1998, *The New York Times* ran an article by Claudia H. Deutsch exploring the issue. The article explores the tension between Wall Street skeptics and the environmentalists who have tried to convince them that a correlation exists between reducing environmental costs and increasing shareholder wealth.[12]

In the article, Matthew J. Kiernan, chief executive of Innovest Strategic Value Advisors in Toronto, said, "Wall Street sees environment as irrelevant, or bad news waiting to happen. We say it is a robust proxy for financial performance."[13]

In another article in *Corporate Environmental Strategy*. Linda Descano and Bradford S. Gentry explore how companies can communicate their environmental performance to the capital markets. Descano is vice president of environmental affairs for Salomon Smith Barney, while Gentry is director of the Research Program on Private Finance and the Environment at the Yale Center for Environmental Law and Policy, and associate director of the Industrial Environmental Management Program at the Yale School of Forestry and Environmental Studies.[14]

They point to "an ever-increasing body of evidence in the business literature" that there is a connection between proactive environmental initiatives and cost opportunities, but often, companies don't know how to convey this information to the market analysts. An analyst will use corporate information to weigh the value of a company, and because much of that information comes from the company itself, many top managers can help themselves by learning how to quantify these savings and communicate them to the analyst. Although financial analysts are beginning to see a link between environmental and financial performance, the companies themselves will have to do a better job of communicating the information analysts need if a real change is to occur, Descano and Gentry conclude.[15]

The EPA's Weiler said if someone were to assemble all the studies and articles, there seems to be some weak evidence that ISO 14001 could some day have a financial payback in terms of bank loans and stock prices. "Never is a very long time," he said, leaving the door open for the future possibility that it could happen. Moreover, there are other more compelling drivers for ISO 14001, he noted.

Notes

1. Smoller, J., telephone interview, January 11, 1999.
2. Zimmerman, M., telephone interview, January 9, 1999.
3. Adrian, J. R., telephone interview, November 4, 1998.
4. Adrian, J. R., slide presentation, Keller Technical Institute's National HazRegs Safety Conference, Chicago, Illinois, November 13, 1998.
5. Ibid.
6. Adrian, telephone interview.
7. Todd, E., telephone interview, January 8, 1999.
8. Weiler, E., telephone interview, January 8, 1999.
9. Ameer, P., Feldman, I., and Soyka, P. A., Does Improving a Firm's Environmental Management System and Environmental Performance Result in a Higher Stock Price?, ICF Kaiser International, Inc., Fairfax, Virginia, 1996.
10. Ibid.
11. Press Release, ICF Kaiser, January 22, 1997, on the web site of The Law Offices of S. Wayne Rosenbaim in Carlsbad, California.
12. Deutsch, C. H., For Wall Street, Increasing Evidence that Green Begets Green, *The New York Times,* July 19, 1998.
13. Ibid.
14. Descano, L., and Gentry, B. S., Communicating Environmental Performance to the Capital Markets, *Corporate Environmental Strategy,* 3(15), 1998.
15. Ibid.

Chapter 8

The Legal Malaise

As standards writers prepare to revise ISO 14001, they undoubtedly will feel intense pressure from a variety of sources to beef up the public reporting requirements in the three-year-old standard. In the fall of 1998, the author attended a SubTAG 1 meeting in Washington, D.C., in which regulators and environmental activists called for more transparency in the standard. If ISO 14001 was to have any credibility, they argued, it needed to be more transparent, requiring a public accounting by companies that decide to certify the standard — especially if those same companies chose to publicize the certification. But industry representatives pointed to the voluntary nature of the standard, saying that ISO 14001 companies are choosing to go above and beyond compliance, so they shouldn't have to reveal confidential information about voluntary, proactive initiatives. After all, they are trying to do more than the law requires of them, they countered. To which ENGOs respond: If industry is not doing anything wrong, why won't it document and report its ISO 14001 activities?

To the author, that question seemed to encapsulate the entire debate, as well as raise other pertinent legal issues surrounding the environmental management system (EMS) standard. According to one leading ISO 14000 attorney, David J. Freeman, the answer to that question is simple — companies have every right to be afraid that public disclosure of ISO 14001 information could be used against them.

"I think that there are very few companies, certainly very few big companies, that can confidently predict that they are complying with every single environmental law and every permit condition," said Freeman, a partner at the New York law firm of Battle Fowler and a former co-chair of the ISO 14000 Legal Issues Forum. "You can have a very good record and still have issues of noncompliance. There are things that (transpire) on the factory floor that top management is unaware of. No matter how good your program is, there is a risk that, when you go out to look at it, you will find something that you do not anticipate."[1]

Companies' legal concerns are more prevalent in the United States, he said, noting that it is a much more litigious society in which potential litigants have greater ability to gain access to documents. In fact, some companies might even shy away from ISO 14001 certification because of the fear of an outside, third party discovering confidential information, he said. "Companies that are very sensitive about confidentiality should consider self-declaration rather than third-party certification," Freeman said. "Self-declaration isn't as credible as the third-party (certification), but you have to make a judgement as to how important that is to your stakeholders. It will be different within industries and between companies. If you are after credibility and willing to take some risks of disclosure, then you go with the third-party certification. If that is not as important to you and you are more sensitive (about exposure), then you might opt for self-declaration."

He continued, "There are certain things you can do to help protect yourself. They are not fictitious fears, but they can be dealt with." Before companies implement a full-fledged ISO system, they ought to do a preliminary audit that can be protected by attorney-client privilege so the companies can discover what their potential exposures are. This audit allows the companies to deal with issues in as confidential a manner as possible while remaining within the law. "The minute you get into an ISO audit, particularly if it is a third-party certification, you run the risk of waiving some privileges. If you know in advance what your exposures are and have dealt with them, then you minimize your risks."

The Third-Party Dilemma

The legal issues surrounding the registration role of the third-party auditor have been debated in ISO circles — including the Legal Issues Forum — for years. The Legal Issues Forum is an organization that meets regularly to dialogue about relevant issues. In fact, the Legal Issues Forum addressed the third-party auditor's role at one of its 1996 meetings near the October 1 release date of the three ISO 14000 auditing standards. According to an article in *International Environmental Systems Update*, some 50 people talked about this issue, raising several pivotal questions:

- Does the auditor look for compliance?
- What does the auditor do if he or she finds noncompliance issues?
- What will be the role of corporate legal counsel?
- Will the EMS audit report reflect the noncompliance? If so, how?
- Does "legal privilege" fit into the noncompliance equation?[2]

While many of those questions persist today, another prominent ISO 14000 attorney said the theoretical issue about third-party auditors' reporting violations has not been a practical problem to date. Another lawyer who is an expert in ISO 14000, William L. Thomas of the Washington law office of Winthrop, Stimson, Putnam & Roberts, said, "Generally, I don't think environmental auditors are running around reporting the violations of their clients to the authorities."[3] Thomas added, however, that "legal factors could play a material part in some companies' decisions not to certify to ISO 14001, though for most firms the choice will be based on other factors, such as competitiveness concerns, market access, shareholder expectations, and the like." But raising the same specter as Freeman, Thomas observed, "If I self-declare, I don't have external auditors attaining access to information that they might subsequently be called upon to disclose during litigation. Self-declaration offers a means of limiting such risk."

Addressing a related legal issue, Freeman noted, "I think that companies are quite concerned about the extent of documentation that is required (with ISO 14001) and the extent, certainly in the United States, that that documentation could find its way into the wrong hands and be used against the company either in an enforcement action or by a governmental agency or some kind of private cause of action, such as toxic torts, property damage, or personal injury. That is one set of issues. A second set is the concern that the implementation of environmental management systems will be thought of as 'state of the art' such that companies that do not have them will have that fact used against them if they get in trouble."

Other legal concerns surrounding ISO 14000 involve the way in which environmental declarations and claims standards interface with the Federal Trade Commission guidelines. To the extent that there are inconsistencies, how will those be addressed? Although ISO 14000 proponents say the EMS series is designed to break trade barriers, another legal issue Freeman identified is whether governmental requirements and supplier requirements related to ISO 14001 could actually result in trade barriers. For example, Freeman said that nobody can predict yet how the ISO 14001 standard is going to play in the international arena. If a supplier in an industrialized country requires adherence to ISO 14001 or a government gives preference to an ISO 14001-certified company in its purchasing decisions, how would that impact a company exporting from a country where it is difficult to become certified because there is a lack of qualified registrars? Because of an insufficient infrastructure, the system could be disadvantaging exporters in a particular country.

Addressing the business advantages of ISO 14001, Freeman said, "I think the major benefit really is that if it is properly implemented, it represents a commitment from top management to developing a system that will be a preventive system, not just a system that responds to regulatory requirements in a reactive mode, but looks holistically at the company's operations and tries to determine what will benefit the environment most in terms of improving the company's operations. In terms of the company's benefit, I think it is the emphasis on awareness and training. One thing that a properly implemented ISO program does is it will reach right down to the factory floor. It will get people involved, get people to think about what they are doing in (terms of) the environmental impact of all their operations, and how that relates to other company processes.

"It is a cross-cutting kind of process that companies go through in setting up these kinds of programs. You will have, again in a well-implemented program, product designers starting to think of the kinds of impacts that a new product design can have on the environment, and be working with the engineers who will be creating the production processes to figure out how to reduce the environmental impact of the new product or design. This is something that in a lot of companies is not happening yet."

Addressing the perceived benefit of regulatory relief, Freeman said that he is disappointed that the regulators have not been more forthcoming in this area. But he quickly added that while regulators may not yet be offering formal regulatory relief, companies perceived as "good actors" are going to get the benefit of the doubt, and the reverse is true for companies perceived to be "bad actors."

"These distinctions that people make in their minds (about companies) can have real consequences," said Freeman, who previously was a regulator and saw things from the other side of the fence.

Government Recognition of EMSs

Freeman pointed to highly publicized court cases in which companies were mandated to implement an ISO 14001 EMS as a result of their settlement with regulators. Those cases are "very significant (because) they represent recognition that the implementation of environmental systems is a benefit to the public. They can be effective in improving environmental quality and reducing issues of noncompliance. Of course, the critics of

ISO 14000 continue to charge that just having an EMS does not guarantee anything about compliance. Maybe that is literally true, but as a practical matter, the fact that the courts are requiring these systems indicates that there is recognition in the real world that environmental management systems are in general beneficial and can have very positive results."

Thomas concurred with Freeman. "Where I see ISO interfacing with my international environmental law practice is in the area of compliance and enforcement," Thomas said. Even though there is ongoing tension over the notion of regulatory relief, Thomas indicated that recent state and federal case settlements are very significant in that the government has imposed ISO 14001 requirements on companies in exchange for resolving alleged statutory violations.

A 1998 settlement involving the mining firm ASARCO was significant because it marked the first government-imposed EMS to extend across a corporation, rather than at a single facility, said Thomas, who participated on an expert panel presentation of the use of Total Quality Environmental Management approaches in enforcement March 31, 1999, at a workshop at the Illinois Environmental Protection Agency in Springfield. In that workshop, he presented a paper on the Role of Pollution Prevention and Environmental Management Systems in Enforcement that included a survey of many recent court-imposed or negotiated arrangements, including ASARCO. In the ASARCO case, the company was alleged to have violated the Clean Water Act and the Resource Conservation and Recovery Act. The consent decree, agreed to in January 1998, contained environmental management and protection requirements designed to enhance ASARCO's corporate-level EMS to "promote compliance," according to Thomas's paper. ASARCO implemented a corporatewide ISO 14001 EMS.

On April 15, 1999, ASARCO and the EPA announced a second agreement that includes consultant requirements and environmental and EMS audit procedures that involve third-parties in the verification process.[4]

Some other noteworthy enforcement cases Thomas highlighted for the Illinois workshop include:

Canada

- Prospec Chemicals, Ltd. in Alberta, allegedly exceeded the allowable air emissions of total reduced sulfur, and in exchange for reduced fines, the company earned an ISO 14001 certification. Prospec beat the court-imposed deadline by three months, earning its certification in March 1998.[5]

- Coretec, Inc. allegedly violated the Canadian Environmental Protection Act and was required by an Ontario court to obtain ISO 14001 certification.

United States

- Hussey Copper, Ltd. in Pennsylvania allegedly violated the state's Solid Waste Management Act, Clean Streams Law, and Administrative Code. The Consent Order required Hussey to contract with a consultant to help the company develop an EMS for the facility. Although the Consent Order had several EMS requirements, it did not mention ISO 14001.
- HCI Chemtech in Missouri pled guilty to criminal felony violations of the Clean Water Act. In addition to its fines and restitution, the company had to commit resources to implementing an EMS that must meet or exceed the specifications of ISO 14001.
- General Motors Corporation in Delaware allegedly violated the state's Code Chapter 60 and Air Pollution Control Regulations and, as a result, the facility must obtain ISO 14001 certification by 2000.
- Reliance Electric-Highland (a division of Rockwell Automation) resolved its dispute with the Indiana Department of Environmental Management by agreeing to pay a civil penalty of $13,922, with $6247 of that amount to be paid in cash. The court also imposed that the company perform and complete a Supplemental Environmental Project (SEP) in lieu of paying the remainder of the civil penalty; the price tag for the SEP is at least $30,000. The SEP includes an agreement to implement an ISO 14001 EMS, requiring certification to the standard.[6]

[For a complete listing of Thomas' survey of court-imposed agreements see Figure 8.1.]

"In Canada, you have two decisions where courts imposed ISO 14001 certification as a prerequisite to a clean record at the end of the day," Thomas said. "The courts gave them a certain time period to do that. In the United States, you see states like Pennsylvania and Delaware imposing EMS obligations. ... What the government is able to say is, 'We have exacted from this polluter a financial penalty, and we have made sure they are on a path that not only will provide compliance but something beyond that.' The 'something beyond that' depends on the environmental management system at issue."[7]

Figure 8.1

COURT-IMPOSED OR NEGOTIATED EMS OBLIGATIONS															
OBLIGATIONS	Prospec	Coretec	Hussey	HCI	ASARCO1	ASARCO2	AWC	Reliance	Nanticoke	Morrell	BNL	Donsco	GM	Keystone	FMC	COMMENTS
ISO 14001 Certification	■	■						■					■			
ISO 14001 Implementation									■	■					■	Donsco had already decided to secure ISO 14001 certification. FMC to implement ISO 14001 principles with enhancements along lines proposed by NEIC.
EMS Implementation			■	■	■		■			■		■		■		ASARCO and Hussey had already decided to implement ISO 14001. EPA could require ISO 14001 after a year if not satisfied with HCI's EMS.
Environmental Metrics Reporting					■		■									

Figure 8.1

In these court cases and the regulatory pilot programs in the states, one can discern a positive connection between strong EMSs and compliance, and even superior performance above the compliance baseline, Thomas said. As the EMS pilot project data is collected by the Multi-State Working Group on Environmental Management Systems (MSWG), he added, the dialogue about how to use EMS measures in enforcement situations will become more nuanced.

"It is not whether enforcement will play a critical role in environmental protection — because it always will. The question, rather, is whether in

COURT-IMPOSED OR NEGOTIATED EMS OBLIGATIONS

OBLIGATIONS	Prospec	Coretec	Hussey	HCI	ASARCO1	ASARCO2	AWC	Reliance	Nanticoke	Morrell	BNL	Donsco	GM	Keystone	FMC	COMMENTS
Technology Transfer					■			■								
Consultant Requirements					■	■	■		■	■		■		■	■	
Third-Party Audit			■		■				■	■					■	ASARCO negotiating agreement w/ EPA incorporating third-party audits. Morrell auditors limited to non-privileged information.
EMS Data Protocols								■				■				
EMS Plan Approval			■	■	■					■		■	■	■		
Pollution Prevention		■	■		■					■		■	■	■		

Source: William L. Thomas, attorney with Winthrop, Stimson, Putnam & Roberts in Washington, D.C. With permission.

Figure 8.1 (continued)

some cases environmental values might best be promoted through the complementary use of EMS concepts and techniques. I think the answer to that question is a resounding 'yes.' "

Thomas pointed to another major area of legal concern related to ISO 14000, describing it as legal/management system convergence. By that, he means things like a range of regulatory regimes that impose management system obligations on firms that have overlapping elements — all of which are premised on the notion that better-managed organizations are more able to avoid accidents, releases, and episodes of noncompliance. For example, Thomas has researched and written extensively about the International Safety Management Code. The ISM Code governs operations in the maritime sector, including oil tankers and passenger cruise ships; it is designed to avoid casualties at sea and oil spills. So a company like Mobil is obligated to have its ships complying with the ISM code. "Such firms must confront the challenge of designing overall approaches that not only satisfy legal obligations, but also other competitive objectives such as adherence to voluntary management systems like ISO 14001," he explained. [For more information on the ISM Code, the reader can check out Thomas' extensive analysis: "Achieving and Maximizing ISM Code Compliance with ISO 14001," *Environmental Quality Management*, John Wiley & Sons, Inc., Summer 1998.]

Much Ado about Nothing?

Experienced practitioners respond that those who criticize attorneys for perpetuating U.S. companies' trepidation about becoming ISO 14001 certified are correct on one level. Some environmental lawyers have come out and said "the sky is falling, the sky is falling with regard to documentation," but those attorneys who have remained involved in ISO 14000 have been more conservative about the nature of the risks, Thomas said. "I don't personally view many of these risks as impediments to implementation of the standard. In some cases, however, such risk could deter a firm from pursuing certification, or inform the scope of the certification or the implementation effort. And that is where legal and business acumen come into play. The beauty of ISO 14001 is that it allows firms to examine their strengths and weaknesses and build packages of systematic improvements to either build on strengths or redress weaknesses. And I think it would be imprudent for firms to be doing that without any attention to the potential legal ramifications of generating certain information, documenting certain events and practices, and setting in place certain standards of conduct."

For these and other legal experts, the conclusion seems to be that while there are significant legal obstacles, companies can address those issues through careful planning and EMS design. Moreover, if properly devised, an ISO 14001 EMS could result in fewer episodes of noncompliance, reduced environmental liabilities, and lower risk of accidents, thereby improving the firm's financial position.

For more information about the potential legal issues arising out of EMS implementation, contact Thomas at (202) 775-9873; fax number: (202) 833-8491. Freeman is available at (212) 856-7126; fax number: (212) 856-7820

Notes

1. Freeman, D. J., telephone interview, January 12, 1999.
2. Legal Issues Forum Addresses the Role of Regulatory Compliance in ISO 14001 Audits, *International Environmental Systems Update,* 10(19), 1996.
3. Thomas, W. L., telephone interview, January 5, 1999.
4. Thomas, W. L., telephone interview, April 22, 1999.
5. Parry, P., Prospec Chemicals Beats Court-Imposed Deadline: Integrated Management System Built from the Bottom Up, *International Environmental Systems Update,* 6(15), 1998.
6. Thomas, W. L., The Role of Pollution Prevention and Environmental Management Systems in Enforcement, presented at the Total Quality Environmental Management Workshop for the Division of Legal Counsel and Compliance Assurance Staff, Illinois Environmental Protection Agency, Springfield, Illinois, March 31, 1999.
7. Thomas, telephone interview.

Chapter 9

On The Horizon

So, why would anyone spend nine months of her life writing a book about the business benefits of ISO 14001? Good question. My mom would like to know. The answer is the same reason why I probably will never write a novel. I like facts. Don't give me theory or platitudes. Simply stick to the facts. After covering ISO 14000 for nearly two years, I thought it was time someone cut through the hope and the hype to ascertain the real benefits of implementing and/or certifying to the international environmental management system standard. I was tired of being bombarded with the "potential benefits" of ISO 14001. I grew weary listening to forecasts of whether the EMS standard would ever attain the same level of acceptance as its popular cousin, ISO 9000. I wanted to move beyond theory and conjecture about the potential impact of the standard to what companies are experiencing in terms of cost savings. I wanted to see if we were putting our money where our proverbial mouth was. Although I readily admit this book has its share of theory and conjecture, the case studies reveal outstanding savings and innovations in waste minimization that provide living models for corporate America and the global community. We put some real dollars and cents to environmental initiatives and talk about return on investment.

Granted, some of the money-saving programs we uncovered don't represent profound thinking. Most of us — if we had given it any thought previously — could have surmised that turning off the lights in the bathroom when it's not in use could save a company money; after all, we do it at home. Also, turning off machinery when a shift is over seems too simple to be translated into big bucks in the bank. But what some companies are saving as a result of energy conservation is startling — and it costs them nothing in terms of capital outlay. Those dollars are real and attainable today. Check your sources of energy and look for areas of conservation.

So, to accomplish the lofty and challenging goal of attaching a dollar value to ISO 14001 initiatives, I set out to compile the best and most recent information. The first thing I did was read, albeit at the speed of light, all the back issues of *International Environmental Systems Update* — the publication of record on ISO 14000, which is published by one of the most reputable companies in this arena. CEEM provides reliable, solid information. The second step was to spend hours on the Internet. The best site for valuable, in-depth information was previously unknown to me, and I discovered it in my research. James Haklik, president of Transformation Strategies in Phoenix, Arizona, runs an ISO 14000 site that contains outstanding material; I spent hours on this site alone. And it's free. Or at least it was during the months I conducted my research. The site can be found at http://www.trst.com. I visited dozens and dozens of other sites. Once I had mounds of material, I interviewed 43 people in person, over the telephone, or via e-mail. I sought those whom I considered to be the best of the best. No one knows more about ISO 14000 than Joe Cascio. ISO 14000 courses through his veins. And few are as bright, straight-spoken, and just plain credible as Marilyn Block. In addition to the consultants, I sought regulators, industry leaders, NGO representatives, registrars, attorneys, economists, and others. Again, only the cream of the crop would do, with the likes of Joe Hess from STMicroelectronics, Jack Bailey at Acushnet Rubber Company, David Schell of Wilton Armetale, and Stephen Evanoff at Lockheed Martin Corporation. Their experiences alone are worth the price of this book. As a bonus, we get a glimpse into Ford's cost savings and what Baxter International has been able to accomplish in terms of waste reduction and its associated savings. Those case studies are transferable and have practical application at virtually any company.

So, amidst all the theories on the viability of the standard, intertwined with solid figures on cost savings, just how do you build a business case for ISO 14001?

In the previous chapters, we've tackled that question from varying vantage points depending on the specialist and the corporation. In our last pages together, we will synthesize those voices and outline, in straight talk, how to do just that. Because every company situation is unique, we'll stick to some general principles learned from those 43 specialists and multiple other sources.

How Do You Build a Business Case for ISO 14001?

If an environmental manager wants to build a business case for ISO 14001, these are the ten steps to take.

1. **Change the way you think.**

   Yes, corporate culture change begins with the environmentalist on staff. You've been driven by compliance for years, and you have to jettison that mentality. Traditionally, you have had to justify any program by demonstrating that you are going to be in better compliance while spending less money. And if that is your frame of reference, you'll never make a business case for ISO 14001, according to some of the consultants.

   Don't misunderstand, we're not suggesting that you can ignore your regulatory obligations to be in compliance, but a business case for ISO 14001 requires a new "paradigm." [Yes, I know, I chose that word carefully. Just be glad we're not thinking outside of the box!]

   Compliance is the floor, not the ceiling, of where companies ought to be headed with their environmental responsibilities. So, you have got to keep that at the forefront. Because if you don't stay on message, you can be sure the employees won't.

2. **Become sophisticated in the ways of ISO 14000.**

   Environmental managers are technical individuals who are used to doing water treatment; they're into filters and pH readings. While ISO 14001 isn't rocket science, it does represent a departure for most environmental managers' frame of reference. So before you can build a business case for senior management, you need to become sophisticated in the ISO 14000 world, which takes us to the next point.

3. **Get outside help.**

   - I'd retain a reputable consultant whose work you trust, but heed the advice of Lee Sanders. She says don't hire someone strictly on reputation. Honda Transmission Manufacturing of America in Ohio lost valuable time and money on its first consultant. When Sanders first began her ISO 14001 journey, it was new and she placed trust in the consultant, whose performance didn't match the reputation. Get evidence of the consultant's competence, perhaps through references of clients, then hire that person.
   - Talk to leaders in the field, such as Bailey and Schell, who have had solid systems in place for years now. Ask them how they

implemented their systems and seek their counsel. After all, Bailey's company saves $2 million annually because of its environmental initiatives. Arm yourself with his case study when you address top management. They'll listen.

- Consider joining a broader group like the U.S. Technical Advisory Group, or your country's equivalent. Participation in the standards development not only gives you a voice, but it provides access to indispensable contacts and information. As a reporter, I am not an apologist for the TAG, nor do I have a vested interest in seeing its membership grow. But if I were a member of industry thinking about implementing ISO 14001, I would want to be a part of that group —even if I was only as a peripheral member.
- Take a reputable ISO 1400 course. A plethora of good, solid course providers exist, and I won't endorse one over another. But the Registrar Accreditation Board (RAB) maintains an EMS course provider database which you can search at http://rab-net.com.

4. **Build upon internal business strategy and structures.**

   ISO 14001 should undergird the company's corporate mission, vision, and business strategy. You need to study all three, and find concrete examples of how ISO 14001 can foster them. Our friends at Lockheed Martin Corporation say they didn't build a traditional business case because they couldn't imagine environmental management not being a part of the overall corporate strategy like other business issues. Block also maintains that environmental decisions should be treated like any other business decision.

5. **If ISO 14001 does not align with your business strategies, don't force it. In fact, don't do it.**

   ISO 14001 should not be pursued because it is a key to the latest international clique. If the global standard does not mesh with your business priorities, don't do it. It's that simple. But according to many of the specialists interviewed, an EMS will be vital to your company's staying power over time. Eventually, you probably will need to implement some system, and ISO 14001 is an internationally recognized standard.

6. **Look for potential cost savings within the corporation.**

   It does not matter where you work; you have waste and inefficiencies in your system. Look for them. Expose them. Then correct them. An EMS will provide the corporate impetus to do this, especially if a third-party registrar is going to audit the facility. Look for the simple, quick fixes first. Then use your imagination to make bigger changes. You might even think outside the box on this one.

7. **Translate environmental initiatives into business language.**
   Learn the foreign language of top management and master it. Talk to them about how ISO 14001 will be good for business and do so in their native tongue.

   For example, a TV commercial running in the United States has a manager asking an employee why the company should go online. The manager asks the employee to explain the reason in terms that senior management can understand. The employee pauses, and then he says, "For every dollar you spend, you'll earn two."

   That's how you talk to management. That's how you sell the business case.

8. **Avoid the strictly-accounting pitfall.**
   But consultants like Cascio warn industry to steer clear of the strictly-accounting approach to the business case, because so many of the EMS standard's benefits are intangible and nearly impossible to quantify. Use the numbers; give them meaning; but go beyond the bottom line to address things like employee morale. A happy workforce is a more productive workforce. A more productive workforce means greater profit, but how much profit, you just can't say. ISO 14001 has so many intangibles that strictly crunching numbers won't sell the standard.

9. **Convince top management that ISO 14001 is one of the best ways to manage your company's impact on the environment — for the long haul.**
   ISO 14001 does not guarantee green products; it doesn't promise cost savings; it even fails to secure compliance. Technically, you can earn a certificate and not be in compliance. Practically, however, you can't stay out of compliance and keep your certificate, but you can probably earn one under some strange circumstance.

   But what ISO 14001 does do is equip the company with a systematic way to approach its environmental responsibilities that will have you soaring past compliance and end-of-pipe issues and thwarting waste at the source.

10. **Brace yourself for change. A successfully implemented ISO 14001 will change your company forever.**

Your company and, in turn, your job will never be the same. One of the potential benefits of ISO 14001 that often gets bandied about is that the EMS makes the environmental managers' job easier because it streamlines the paperwork. I could not find much support for that theory in my research. Yes, some environmental managers probably have benefitted from a reduction in paperwork. Some benefitted from having a better system of documentation. But others say that ISO 14001 documentation requirements have increased the amount of papers they shuffle on their desks.

One environmental manager I spoke with phrased it best. He said that implementing ISO 14001 does not make his job easier, per se, but it does make it more secure and more precise. Before his company implemented ISO 14001, he was responsible for environmental obligations as the "environmental guy." But now, environmental stewardship is seen as the duty and responsibility of every employee at his firm. Because ISO 14001 requires employee awareness of the standard and the company's environmental policy, employees undergo rigorous training in preparation for the audit and to ensure continuous improvement of the system. Having a corporatewide responsibility means it is less likely that environmental manager will bear the blame alone if an incident occurs. Also, involvement of all the employees can create a synergy in which new ideas and programs come to the forefront that otherwise would never have materialized. If you implement ISO 14001, your job will change — you will have to share the responsibility for the environment with all of your co-workers.

What's in Store for the New Millennium?

As this century comes to a close, some within the standards industry are awaiting many changes on the horizon. ISO 9000 is in the middle of a revisions process, which is expected to culminate in the new millennium. Typically, ISO standards are revised or at least revisited every five years, but there's movement afoot to fast-track ISO 14001 so that greater compatibility can be achieved between the two standards. But how things will exactly unfold is anybody's guess.

As tempting as it is to make predictions — after all, the advent of a new millennium often attracts prophets — I refuse to do so. I don't know if we'll get all the bugs out of the Y2K computer problem in time. I don't know if the Democrats will retain the White House. And I sure don't know if we'll ever solve the mystery behind the JFK assassination. So, why would I predict the future viability of ISO 14001? I stick to the facts, remember?

What I can do is offer some observations based on research and the insight of my sources. You can draw your own conclusions and make your own predictions.

First, ISO 14001 may gain the same level of acceptance as ISO 9000. More than 10,000 certificates have been issued worldwide at the time of this writing, and in some corners of the world, like Asia, the EMS standard is a hot commodity. As more global companies like IBM and Bristol-Myers Squibb encourage the greening of their supply chains, the standard has a better shot of becoming an international sensation. And just like in political races, ISO 14001 might even ride the coattails of ISO 9000, as it is the quality management system standard that put the Geneva-based ISO on the map.

But then again, it might not happen. Why? Well, for one thing, we don't have enough implementation experience to make assessments as to the durability of the standard. But, as we've seen through the past several hundred pages, ISO 14001 seems to be potent in the companies in which it has been successfully implemented. The truth is that ISO 9000 may always be more popular. For one thing, companies always understand the value of having a quality management system in place that should translate into better business practices. And some companies may always view the environment as a necessary evil — something that costs them money but must be dealt with to keep them two steps ahead of the regulators. It's hard for some in industry to see the EMS standard could be as valuable to the business as the QMS standard.

Forgive the cliché, but only time will tell.

Second, the biggest issue facing the young EMS standard is one of credibility. And frankly, this issue will decide the fate of the first question we've just discussed. ISO 14001 must overcome its credibility issue to reach its full viability. Key to the credibility issue is the transparency of the standard and the distrust between the primary actors. Industry would like to use ISO 14001 as a tool to help it be in compliance and then go beyond the law to new heights. And as such, industry would like to see the revisions of ISO 14001 kept at bay until its representatives have had enough time to study implementation results. Frankly, some members of industry told me they felt they were deserving of trust as they have sought to be environmental stewards. While not voicing it, some of their tone was resentful and, yes, even a bit hurt that members of the regulatory community and NGOs don't trust them. After all, why would they be so involved in ISO 14001 if they didn't care about the environment?

On the other hand, NGOs and regulators have said that some minor language changes in ISO 14001 could only strengthen it by addressing public reporting issues. The bottom line is NGOs are afraid. They don't want to hurt the world by misplacing their trust. And regulators are trapped in a political climate that feeds off distrust. Even if both groups did trust proactive companies like the ones in this book, they cannot afford to let their guards down for the thousands of companies that they don't know about. And even if they did, the regulatory web remains.

The most crucial, pressing issue for the viability of ISO 14001 today is for these three camps to come together and, yes, even for them to trust one another. And great strides toward this end has been made in the U.S. Technical Advisory Group, where representatives of all three segments work together to affect change. TAG members work together as colleagues — even if this political wall remains. Frankly, I have no sense that this wall can ever come down. At the risk of sounding like a candidate for political office, the rub exists because all three groups are right. Some members of industry do deserve our trust. NGOs can't get caught napping. And regulators have a job to do.

So, the question remains: Where does that leave ISO 14001?

The truth is, we don't know. What we do know is that ISO 14001 has prospered in the last three years, saving companies across the globe millions. And for those who have chosen to implement the EMS standard, business benefits — beyond just the intangible — have ensued.

Appendix A

Sample Corporate Environmental Policies

One of the early steps in implementing an ISO 14001 environmental management system (EMS) is the development of the environmental policy. Once the statement is adopted, the company must then train its employees so that everyone is aware of the policy statement. The following EMS statements, which are used with the companies' permission, provide some examples of existing environmental policy statements.

Acushnet Rubber Company

To ensure employees', company's, and society's sustainability, Acushnet Rubber Company is committed to develop and maintain a management system that integrates sound business practices with environmental, safety, health, and quality objectives. These objectives will be reviewed and updated periodically.

Acushnet Rubber Company will strive for continual improvement in all activities with focus on prevention of pollution, life cycle analysis, and toxic use reduction techniques. Acushnet Rubber Company will work with governmental and non-governmental agencies including vendors, research organizations, the local community, and customers to improve product and processes so as to reduce their environmental, safety, and health impact. Acushnet Rubber Company will promote responsible and accurate statements of its product while avoiding false or misleading claims of quality, safety, health, or environmental benefits. Acushnet Rubber Company will comply with all federal, state and city regulations.

Signed by,

Ron Parrish, CEO

Ron Fernandes, Executive Vice President

Jack Bailey, EHS Director*

Baxter International, Inc.

Baxter will be a global leader in Environmental, Health and Safety (EHS) management. This is consistent with Baxter's business interests, ethics and shared values.

Specifically, we commit to the following:

Sustainable Development — We will strive to conserve resources and minimize or eliminate adverse EHS effects and risks that may be associated with our products, services and operations.

Employees — We will provide a safe and healthy workplace, striving to prevent injuries and illnesses, promoting healthy lifestyles and encouraging respect for the environment. We will ensure that our employees have the awareness, skills and knowledge to carry out this policy.

Compliance — We will meet all applicable EHS laws and Baxter EHS requirements, including our own EHS management standards.

Business Integration — We will integrate EHS considerations into our business activities.

Customers — We will work with our customers to help them address their EHS needs.

Suppliers and Contractors — We will work with our suppliers and contractors to enhance EHS performance.

Community and Government — We will participate in community and government EHS initiatives.

Baxter commits to continuous improvement in environmental, health and safety performance. We will set goals, measure progress and communicate results. Compliance with this policy is the responsibility of every employee. [Adopted August 4, 1997.]**

Signed by,

---

* From: Acushnet Rubber Company's web site http://www.acushnet.com. With permission.

Vernon R. Loucks Jr., Chairman and Chief Executive Officer

Martha R. Ingram, Chair, Public Policy Committee of the Board of Directors; Chairman and Chief Executive Officer, Ingram Industries, Inc.

William R. Blackburn, Vice President and Chief Counsel, Corporate Environmental, Health and Safety

Ford Motor Company

Sustainable economic development is important to the welfare of the company, as well as to society. To be sustainable, economic development must provide protection of human health and the world's environmental resource base. It is Ford's policy that its operations, products and services accomplish their functions in a manner that provides responsibly for protection of health and the environment.

Ford is committed to meeting regulatory requirements that apply to its businesses. With respect to health and environmental concerns, regulatory compliance represents a minimum. When necessary and appropriate, we establish and comply with standards of our own, which may go beyond legal mandates. In seeking appropriate ways to protect health or the environment, the issue of cost alone does not preclude consideration of possible alternatives, and priorities are based on achieving the greatest anticipated practical benefits while striving for continuous improvement.

Ford's policy of responsibly protecting health and the environment is based on the following principles:

Protection of health and the environment is an important consideration in business decisions. Consideration of potential health and environmental effects — as well as present and future regulatory requirements — is an early, integral part of the planning process. Company products, services, processes and facilities are planned and operated to incorporate objectives and targets that are periodically reviewed to minimize to the extent practical the creation of waste, pollution and any adverse impact on health and the environment. Protection of health and the environment is a companywide responsibility. Management of each activity is expected to accept this responsibility as an important priority and to commit the necessary resources. Employees at all levels are expected to carry out this responsibility as part of their particular assignments and to cooperate in company efforts.

** From: Baxter International's 1997 Environmental Health & Safety Performance Report, Issued in 1998. With permission.

The adoption and enforcement of responsible, effective and sound laws, regulations, policies and practices protecting health and the environment are in the company's interest. Accordingly, we participate constructively with government officials, private organizations, and concerned members of the general public. Likewise, it is in our interest to provide timely and accurate information to our publics on environmental matters involving the company.*

Honda Transmission Manufacturing of America

HTM will commit to the protection of the environment in all areas of operation. HTM recognizes its obligations as a responsible corporate citizen and as such will conduct its manufacturing operations according to the following principles:

- HTM will comply with all applicable environmental requirements as mandated by federal, state and local law.
- HTM will comply with all internal policies regarding protection of the environment.
- HTM will commit to developing processes and practices to reduce pollution and conserve natural resources.
- HTM will develop an Environmental Management System to monitor and control environmental impacts of our operations.
- HTM is committed to the requirements of ISO 14001 and other programs to which HTM subscribes.

HTM Environmental Policy and business planning process will provide a base for establishing and reviewing environmental goals and objectives for the purposes of continuous improvement. [Revised 4/23/98.]**

The John Roberts Company

The John Roberts Company is committed to managing all of its operations in an environmentally sound manner. We intend to involve our employees, our suppliers and our customers in the principle that to conduct business at the expense of the environment around us is simply unacceptable.

---

* From: Ford Motor Company's 1998 Environmental Report. With permission.
** From: Honda Transmission Manufacturing of America. With permission.

Through awareness, understanding, education and action we will minimize our intrusion on the environment.*

---

* From: *International Environmental Systems Update,* July 1998, page 16. With permission.

Appendix B

EPA Position Statement on ISO 14000

Federal Register: March 12, 1998 (Volume 63, Number 48)
Notices • Pages 12,094-12,097
Source: From the Federal Register Online via GPO Access
[wais.access.gpo.gov]

Environmental Protection Agency

EPA Position Statement on Environmental Management Systems and ISO 14001 and a Request for Comments on the Nature of the Data To Be Collected From Environmental Management System/ISO 14001 Pilots

ACTION: Position statement; request for comment on information gathering.

SUMMARY: This document communicates the EPA's position regarding Environmental Management Systems (EMSs), including those based on the International Organization for Standardization (ISO) 14001 standard. This document also describes the evaluative stage EPA is entering concerning EMSs. Further, it solicits comments on proposed categories of information to be collected from a variety of sources that will provide data for a public policy evaluation of EMSs.

For Further Information Contact:

Office of Reinvention — EMS, Environmental Protection Agency
401 M St., SW, mail code 1803, Washington, D.C. 20460
Telephone: (202) 260-4261
E-mail: reinvention@epamail.epa.gov.

Supplementary Information:

I. Background

A diverse group of organizations, associations, private corporations and governments has been developing and implementing various EMS frameworks for the past thirty years. For example, the Chemical Manufacturers Association created its own framework called Responsible Care. In addition, the French, Irish, Dutch, and Spanish governments developed their own voluntary EMS standards.

The possibility that these diverse EMS frameworks could result in barriers to international trade led to a heightened interest in formulating an international voluntary standard for EMSs. To that end, the International Organization for Standardization (ISO), consisting of representatives from industry, government, non-governmental organizations (NGOs), and other entities, finalized the ISO 14001 EMS standard in September 1996. The intent of this standard is to produce a single framework for EMSs, which can accommodate varied applications all over the world. ISO 14001 is unique among the ISO 14000 standards because it can be objectively audited against for internal evaluation purposes or for purposes of self-declaration or third-party certification of the system.

EPA participation in the development of voluntary standards, including the ISO 14000 series of standards, is consistent with the goals reflected in section 12(d) of the National Technology Transfer and Advancement Act of 1995 (NTTAA) (Pub. L. No. 104-113, s. 12(d), 15 U.S.C. 272 note). The NTTAA requires federal agencies to use voluntary consensus standards in certain activities as a means of carrying out policy objectives or other activities determined by the agencies, unless the use of these standards would be inconsistent with applicable law or otherwise impractical. In addition, agencies must participate in the development of voluntary standards when such participation is in the public interest and is compatible with an agency's mission, authority, priority, and budget resources. Agency participation in the development of EMS voluntary standards does not necessarily connote EPA's agreement with, or endorsement of, such voluntary standards. On December 16, 1997, EPA Deputy Administrator Fred Hansen asked EPA's newly chartered Office of Reinvention "to take lead responsibility for policy coordination of all EMS pilots, programs, and communications." This notice initiates the Office of Reinvention's effort to ensure public input in that endeavor. (See complete memorandum published in Appendix C.)

II. Statement

Implementation of an EMS has the potential to improve an organization's environmental performance and compliance with regulatory requirements. EPA supports and will help promote the development and use of EMSs, including those based on the ISO 14001 standard, that help an organization achieve its environmental obligations and broader environmental performance goals. In doing so, EPA will work closely with all key stakeholders, especially our partners in the States.

EPA encourages the use of EMSs that focus on improved environmental performance and compliance as well as source reduction (pollution prevention) and system performance. EPA supports efforts to develop quality data on the performance of any EMS to determine the extent to which the system can help bring about improvements in these areas. EPA also encourages organizations that develop EMSs to do so through an open and inclusive process with relevant stakeholders, and to maintain accountability for the performance outcomes of their EMSs through measurable objectives and targets. EPA encourages organizations to make information on the actual performance of their environmental management systems available to the public and governmental agencies. In addition, through initiatives such as Project XL and the Environmental Leadership Program, EPA is encouraging the testing of EMSs to achieve superior environmental performance. At this time, EPA is not basing any regulatory incentives solely on the use of EMSs, or certification to ISO 14001.

The Commission for Environmental Cooperation (CEC) Council issued on June 12, 1997, a resolution (#97-05) signed by EPA Deputy Administrator Fred Hansen on behalf of the United States concerning "future cooperation regarding environmental management systems and compliance." The CEC Council was formed pursuant to the North American Agreement on Environmental Cooperation, an environmental side agreement to the North American Free Trade Agreement, and is comprised of the environmental

ministers for Canada, Mexico and the United States. The declarative and directive paragraphs of the Council's resolution #97-05 read as follows:
The Council Declares That:

> Governments must retain the primary role in establishing environmental standards and verifying and enforcing compliance with laws and regulations. Strong and effective governmental programs to enforce environmental laws and regulations are essential to ensure the protection of public health and the environment. Voluntary compliance programs and initiatives developed by governments can supplement strong and effective enforcement of environmental laws and regulations, can encourage mutual trust between regulated entities and government, and can facilitate the achievement of common environmental protection goals; Private voluntary efforts, such as adoption of Environmental Management Systems (EMSs) such as those based on the International Organization on Standardization's Specification Standard 14001 (ISO 14001), may also foster improved environmental compliance and sound environmental management and performance. ISO 14001 is not, however, a performance standard.
>
> Adoption of an EMS pursuant to ISO 14001 does not constitute or guarantee compliance with legal requirements and will not in any way prevent the governments from taking enforcement actions where appropriate;
>
> Hereby Directs:
>
> The Working Group to explore (1) the relationship between the ISO 14000 series and other voluntary EMSs to government programs to enforce, verify and promote compliance with environmental laws and regulations, and (2) opportunities to exchange information and develop cooperative positions regarding the role and effect of EMSs on compliance and other environmental performance. The Working Group shall, no later than the 1998 Council Session, report its results to the Council and provide recommendations for future cooperative action in this area. The review and recommendations shall recognize and respect each Party's domestic requirements and sovereignty.

III. Evaluative Phase

EPA is working in partnership with a number of states to explore the utility of EMSs, especially those based substantially on ISO 14001, in public policy innovation. The goal of this partnership is to gather credible and compatible information of known quality adequate to address key public policy issues. The primary mechanism to generate this information will be pilot projects. Valid, compatible data from other sources will also be used whenever possible. To make efficient use of resources, and to ensure more robust research, EPA and states will work together on the creation of a common database. The database will be open and usable, while recognizing the need to insure the appropriate level of confidentiality for participants.

A group of federal and state officials involved in EMS pilot projects have been working together to set up a common national database of information gathered through the pilot projects. As part of that process, EPA and states are developing a series of data protocols which provide instructions and survey instruments to guide the actual collection of data for the database. That document will be available at http://www.epa.gov/reinvent.

This document will serve to solicit comments on the categories of information to be collected. From the following general categories of information (and possibly others), EPA and participating states will develop the above mentioned protocols.

The following categories are designed to provide a general idea as to the types of information that EPA believes should be collected to evaluate the effectiveness of EMSs from the perspective of regulators. EPA further believes that collection of data in all categories will allow the fullest understanding and evaluation of the benefits of an EMS. The data categories which appear in this document were, to the extent possible, developed around the kinds of data we believe will or could be generated by an ISO 14001 EMS.

1. Environmental Performance

The impact a facility has on the environment is of paramount importance to regulators' assessment of EMSs. Thus, it is critical to measure any change in a facility's environmental performance that might be attributable to implementation of an EMS. Information would be collected as to the types, amounts, and properties of pollutants that are released to air, surface water, groundwater, or the land. Information on these pollutants would need to be normalized to a facility's production levels. Information relating to recycling, reuse, and energy requirements could also be included. This inquiry could include both regulated and non-regulated pollutants.

2. Compliance

Implementation of an EMS has the potential to improve an organization's environmental compliance with regulatory requirements. The goal of collecting compliance information is to be able to measure the relationship between an EMS and compliance with local, state and federal environmental regulations. The types of data to be collected would include: information on whether the facility has a recent history of regulatory violations; the number, and seriousness of the violations; how quickly violations were discovered and corrected; and measurements of any changes in regulatory compliance status.

3. Pollution Prevention

Pollution prevention is a significant goal for both federal and state regulators. Therefore, better understanding the relationship between an organization's overall performance and the role of pollution prevention in the organization's EMS is important to regulators. In the federal context, pollution prevention is defined as "any practice which — (i) reduces the amount of any hazardous substance, pollutant, or contaminant entering any waste stream, or otherwise released into the environment (including fugitive emissions) prior to recycling, treatment, or disposal; and (ii) reduces the hazards to public health and the environment associated with the release of such substances, pollutants, or contaminants." [The definition comes from Pollution Prevention Act of 1990 Section 6603, 42 U.S.C. 13102 (1990).] This definition will likely serve as a basis for helping an organization identify measures that it might have taken towards pollution prevention. Data collected would include a description of the type of pollution prevention and source reduction techniques used, including good operating practices, inventory control, spill and leak prevention, raw material modification/substitution, process modification, and product reformulation or redesign.

4. Environmental Conditions

In order to understand the impact of an EMS on the environment, it is necessary to know something about the status of the ambient environment surrounding the facility prior to implementation of an EMS. An analysis of this nature will not only help regulators evaluate EMS, it should also help facility managers prioritize their environmental aspects and shape the policies and objectives of their EMSs. Environmental conditions data will assist all parties in determining the sustainability of certain human activities from an environmental, economic and social perspective. It is difficult, of course, to collect accurate and comparable information about environmental conditions. The time and expense needed for a facility to collect and report such data could be prohibitive. Also, the selection of an appropriate geographic focus — local, regional, or global — will be challenging. One way to minimize this burden would be to utilize available governmental or other surveys (e.g., the 1990 U.S. Census, hydrogeologic reports). Nevertheless, to the degree that these obstacles can be overcome, the analysis conducted by federal and state regulators will benefit.

5. Costs/Benefits to Implementing Facilities

There has been much speculation and assertion about the relative costs and benefits associated with the implementation of an EMS. Data collected in this category should help provide answers to questions concerning possible net financial benefits that might accompany improved compliance and increased environmental performance, or that might result from being able to achieve compliance in less costly ways. The data may also shed light on the costs associated with higher levels of environmental performance. It is important to recognize some of the limitations inherent in traditional approaches to cost/benefit analysis. To address these limitations, organizations could be encouraged to identify intangible costs and benefits associated with the implementation of an EMS, even if they are difficult to quantify. Also, a list of usually "hidden" costs and benefits could be used to help organizations identify and understand costs and benefits that are traditionally overlooked.

6. Stakeholder Participation and Confidence

Community participation has become an increasingly important component of federal and state efforts to increase environmental performance and protect human health. Both federal and state regulators are interested in understanding the involvement of local communities and other stakeholders in the EMS process. Data could be collected to assess the amount and degree of stakeholder participation in both the development and implementation of an organization's EMS, or the effect that such participation has on the public credibility of the facility's EMS implementation.

More information concerning the pilot projects as well as other federal, state and international initiatives relating to EMSs and ISO 14000 can be found in the ISO 14000 Resource Directory [copies can be obtained through EPA's Pollution Prevention Information Clearinghouse at 202-260-1023, e-mail: ppic@epamail.epa.gov].

Dated: March 6, 1998.
Fred Hansen,
Deputy Administrator.

Appendix C

Memo on Coordination of EPA Activities Involving EMSs

December 16, 1997

MEMORANDUM

Subject: Coordination of EPA Programs Involving
Environmental Management Systems

To: Assistant Administrators
General Counsel
Inspector General
Chief Financial Officer
Associate Administrators
Regional Administrators
Staff Office Directors

Much innovative work is underway around the Agency involving voluntary environmental management systems (EMS). EPA is evaluating the use of EMS in a variety of applications, including possible future use in environmental policy decisions. The emergence of a new international standard for EMS, ISO 14001, makes EPA's work in this area all the more timely. Growing numbers of U.S. organizations are using EMS for economic, trade and other competitive benefits along with environmental improvements. EPA pilots and programs which make use of EMS are focused primarily on evaluating how, and how reliably, these EMS might help achieve environmental benefits.

I support this work and want it to continue. I believe implementation of EMSs offers the potential to improve an organization's overall environmental performance, especially through pollution prevention and improved compliance with environmental regulations. At the same time, the number of EMS projects EPA is conducting to explore this potential, and the fact that much of our EMS work involves taking positions in multi-party working groups, suggests a need for strong coordination. EPA must ensure that consistent principles and objectives govern our work and communications with other entities in this arena.

To strengthen and unify our approach to EMS, I have asked Chuck Fox, Associate Administrator for Reinvention, to take lead responsibility for policy coordination of all EMS pilots, programs and communications. The Office of Reinvention, working with the guidance of a cross-Agency team of office directors and senior representatives from Regions, will ensure policy consistency among all EMS activities, and will encourage innovative and credible partnerships with the states and with the private sector. Because ISO 14001 is a voluntary consensus standard, the policy team will also include the EPA Standards Executive, who is responsible for coordinating the Agency's participation in voluntary consensus standards bodies under the National Technology Transfer and Advancement Act.

Where the Voluntary Standards Network (VSN) is addressing EMS, it will operate under the policy guidance of OR. It will continue its excellent work as the principal vehicle for coordinating input to the U.S. Technical Advisory Group on ISO 14000, and will help communicate EPA policies on EMS more broadly. The chairmanship of the VSN will remain in the Office of Prevention, Pesticides, and Toxic Substances.

Early in the new year, the Office of Reinvention (is) to provide me with a status report and briefing that defines EPA's policy approach on EMS and the processes by which its activities will be coordinated — inside the Agency, with State partners, and all other stakeholders. I am especially interested in:

- Publication of the Agency's current position and strategy regarding EMS.

- A plan showing how EMS activities are consistent with our position and integrated in support of our strategy.
- The EPA/State plan for the joint collection, management and analysis of data being developed to test whether EMS lead to improved performance.

Environmental management systems hold great promise for improving environmental conditions in the United States and internationally. I look forward to being involved in EPA's efforts to help realize the full potential of EMS.

Fred Hansen
Deputy Administrator

Source: From <http://www.epa.gov/reinvent/ems/emsmem1.htm>, posted September 14, 1998.

Statement of Principles on Revisions to ISO 14001 U.S. Environmental Protection Agency

November 19, 1998

Background and Purpose

ISO 14001, the international voluntary standard for environmental management systems, was published in Fall, 1996. U.S. EPA was pleased to participate actively in the U.S. Technical Advisory Group (TAG) as the standard was developed and offer suggestions in several important areas that were ultimately supported by the TAG, primarily relating to the roles of pollution prevention and compliance management. We look forward to continuing our involvement in this and other standards-related activities.

EPA's current position statement on EMSs and ISO 14001, which was published in the *Federal Register* on March 12, 1998, makes it clear that the Agency "supports and will help promote the development and use of EMSs, including those based

163

on the ISO 14001 standard, that help an organization achieve its environmental obligations and broader environmental performance goals." Consistent with this statement, EPA is not providing regulatory flexibility at this time for organizations based solely on implementing an EMS, including those based on ISO 14001, nor does our participation in the revisions process imply a commitment to reduce regulatory requirements or take enforcement actions, when necessary, based on modifications to the standard. Any consideration of the role of EMSs, including those based on ISO 14001, in public policy, will take place separately from the formal process for considering revisions to the standard.

Under ISO procedures, all standards are to be reviewed every five years to determine the need for any revisions. The current schedule adopted by ISO's Technical Committee 207 calls for this review to begin at the international level in mid-1999. Revisions to ISO 14001, if any, are not expected to be incorporated into the standard before 2001.

EPA has gained considerable practical experience with EMSs through national and regional initiatives and through their use in enforcement settlements. In partnership with the States, we are sponsoring a number of pilot projects designed to evaluate the effectiveness of EMSs based substantially on ISO 14001. We are also actively supporting the use of EMSs based on ISO 14001 in the public sector, especially with municipalities. This work will be very important in helping to determine the role that ISO 14001 will have in public policy decisions and it will continue. However, discussions of possible revisions to the standard should not be delayed pending receipt of information from these projects.

An Agency workgroup, co-chaired by the Office of Water and EPA Region I, has been formed to coordinate Agency views on the review and possible revisions to ISO 14001. This workgroup has initiated and will continue discussions with States, industry, and non-governmental organizations (NGOs) to better understand their views on the need for revisions to the standard.

This workgroup will serve as the vehicle for communicating official EPA positions regarding the review and revision of ISO 14001.

Recently, a number of questions have been raised concerning EPA's participation in the upcoming review process. The purpose of this document is to describe a series of principles and other important considerations that will govern EPA's participation.

Principles

- EPA will continue to participate actively in the formal process for reviewing ISO 14001 through the U.S. TAG and will consult informally with other stakeholders to better understand their views throughout the review process. It is our hope and expectation that the process adopted by the U.S.

TAGforreviewingthestandardwillbecompletelyopenandwillmaximize the ability of all stakeholders to offer their views on a continuing basis.

- EPA's participation in the revisions process for ISO 14001 is consistent withtheobligationssetoutforFederalagenciesintheNationalTechnology TransferandAdvancementAct(NTTAA)andisbasedontherecognition that the use of EMSs based on ISO 14001 has the potential to improve environmental performance independent of the regulatory process.
- As previously mentioned, EPA is directly implementing or funding a numberofpilotprojects,inpartnershipwithStatesandotherentities.We expect these projects to yield much valuable information on ISO 14001 implementationovertime.However,asstatedabove,discussionsofsome ofthekeyissuesandpossiblerevisionstoISO14001shouldnotbedelayed pending receipt of information from these projects.
- Recognizing that the U.S. TAG is the official forum for developing the U.S. position on possible ISO 14001 revisions, EPA has identified the following issues as warranting discussion for possible modification or clarification of the standard:
  — The relationship of ISO 14001 to regulatory compliance and performance
  — The definition of prevention of pollution
  — Public communications
- Legitimate concerns about these areas have been consistently raised by many organizations in the U.S. and around the world since the developmentofISO14001.Theissuesarenotnewandafullandopendiscussion intheU.S.isneedednowthroughtheU.S.TAG.Thisdiscussionhasbegun and the U.S. TAG has already identified these issues as needing further discussion.

EPA's participation in this discussion will be driven by a goal of maximizing the environmental benefits of the standard, including its ability to address environmental impacts not subject to regulation. This can only happen if the standard is widely adopted by many different types of organizations, including those in the public sector. EPA shares the view that the standard should not be revised in a mannerthatwillmakeitunacceptabletoasignificantnumberofpotentialusers.

Appendix E

Multi-State Working Group on Environmental Management Systems, Robert Stephens, Chair

STATEMENT ON ISO 14001 REVISIONS

March 23, 1998. With permission.

TheMulti-StateWorkingGroup(MSWG)onEnvironmentalManagementSystems welcomes the opportunity to enter into the discussion on potential revisions to the ISO 14001 environmental management system standard. MSWG shares the U.S. TAG's goal of implementing ISO 14000 to achieve environmental improve-mentsandeconomicbenefits.However,toachievethesegoals,anunderstandable andcredibleISO14000systemisrequired,especiallyintheU.S.whereadoption isslowandsomeskepticismexistsamongregulatorsandpublicinterestparties.

Accordingly,theMSWGrecommendsthattheU.S.TAGcreateacollaborative processtoaddressissuesrelatedtoareaswherethestandardmightbeenhancedor clarifiedwhichwouldpotentiallyachievegreaterISO14000credibilityhereand abroad.Webelievethisprocessshouldcommencepromptlyandbebroughttothe TC207.TheMSWG'srecommendationisbasedonnearlytwoyearsofgrassroots discussion involving business, government and non-government interests.

As is known by the U.S. TAG, MSWG's state and federal regulators are commencing pilot projects to test ISO's value in meeting public policy goals. Our pre-test dialogue caused us to conclude that the opportunity for success for ISO 14001 gaining acceptance with a broad community of stakeholders would be greatly enhanced if there were clarification of intent in a few key areas. Accordingly, we recommend the U.S. TAG create a structure and process to address three issues:

1. Public communication relating to setting goals and reporting performance
2. The relationship of the EMS to regulatory compliance and performance regarding all significant environmental aspects
3. The definition of pollution prevention and its role in all aspects of the system

We do not pre-judge the content of the clarifications in each category. However, each deserves a focus that allows private and public interest sectors an opportunity to produce recommended revisions.

Attention to the three areas can be viewed as addressing an opportunity. We, the members of MSWG, believe the full value of all the strategic environmental management represented by the ISO standards cannot be realized without the confidence and support of the public sector. No sector interests are served by creating replicate and separate environmental management systems, one private and one public. We have been coordinating closely with the U.S. EPA on the nexus between the ISO 14000 standards and public confidence and agency programs. This coordination has resulted in formal agreements between the MSWG and the U.S. EPA. There is a consensus between MSWG and EPA as to the importance of addressing the three areas of the standard listed above. It is for these reasons that we encourage the U.S. TAG to assume a leadership position in addressing those issues which could lead to a broader acceptance of the standard.

Paradoxically, the opportunity also is rooted in ISO's credibility among regulators and public interest groups and the political community that is sensitive to both. By producing credible clarity in the three areas, the U.S. TAG can transform a threat into an opportunity and hold out the potential of future attention to the regulatory framework.

We understand some may prefer to wait. This is unwise on its merits and because others outside the U.S. are similarly concerned. So, we need to prepare in anticipation of their positions and actions.

The MSWG thanks the U.S. TAG for this opportunity to communicate its views and is prepared to assist in this process, drawing upon its considerable experience.

Appendix F

Frequently Asked Questions About ISO 14000

[From CEEM, Inc.'s web site: www.ceem.com, 1997. With Permission.]

1. What is ISO?
2. What are the ISO 14000 series standards?
3. How did this effort get started?
4. What is TC 207?
5. What are EMAR and EMAS?
6. What is the U.S. TAG?
7. What is ISO 14001?
8. What is the ISO 14004 guidance document?
9. What are the ISO 14020 labeling standards?
10. What is the ISO 14031 environmental performance evaluation standard?
11. What are the ISO 14040 life-cycle assessment standards?
12. What is the relationship between ISO 14000 and ISO 9000?
13. What is a certification body and what is certification?
14. What's the difference among accreditation, certification, and registration?

15. How much does certification cost?
16. How can I prepare for ISO 14000?

1. What is ISO?

The International Organization for Standardization (ISO) is a worldwide federation founded in 1947 to promote the development of international manufacturing, trade and communication standards. ISO is comprised of member bodies from some 120 countries. The American National Standards Institute (ANSI) is the United States representative to ISO.

ISO receives input from government, industry and other interested parties before developing a standard. All standards developed by ISO are voluntary; no legal requirements force countries to adopt them. However, countries and industries often adopt ISO standards as requirements for doing business, thereby making them virtually mandatory. ISO develops standards in all industries except those related to electrical and electronic engineering. The International Electrotechnical Commission (IEC), which has more than 40 member countries, including the United States, develops standards in these areas.

2. What are the ISO 14000 series standards?

ISO 14000 is a series of voluntary generic standards being developed by ISO that provides business management with the structure for managing environmental impacts. The standards include a broad range of environmental management disciplines, including the basic management system, auditing, performance evaluation, labeling and life-cycle assessment. ISO has assigned responsibility for the standards' development to Technical Committee (TC) 207, which is made-up of subcommittees (SCs) and their working groups (WGs), each assigned a set of related standards. The standards basically are two types: guidance and specification. All the standards except ISO 14001 are guidance standards. This means that they are descriptive documents, rather than prescriptive requirements. A company or an organization does not register to ISO 14000 as a series; it registers to ISO 14001, the specification standard that is a model for an environmental management system. Classified according to their focus, the standards fall into two categories.

1. Organization or process standards — environmental management system (EMS), environmental auditing (EA) and environmental performance evaluation (EPE); and

2. Product-oriented standards — life-cycle assessment (LCA), environmental labeling (EL) and environmental aspects in product standards (EAPS). The EMS and auditing standards became full international standards in September and October 1996, respec-

tively. The other standards are being developed at a varying pace.

3. How did this effort get started?

Some observers trace the genesis of the ISO 14000 series to the 1972 United Nations Conference on Human Environment in Stockholm, which ultimately spawned a 1987 report titled "Our Common Future." This report contained the initial reference to "sustainable development," calling for industry to develop effective environmental management systems. By the end of 1988, more than 50 world leaders had publicly supported the report. The United Nations (U.N.) then convened the U.N. Conference on Environment and Development — the Earth Summit — in Rio de Janeiro in June 1992. In part to prepare for this summit, in 1991 ISO established the Strategic Advisory Group on the Environment (SAGE) to make recommendations regarding international standards.

Efforts to create a single, generic, internationally recognized EMS standard had been driven by the desire among companies to avoid duplicative — and sometimes competitive — corporate and governmental programs and by their need for objective validation of their commitment. Such efforts began on several fronts, but one led the way to ISO 14001.

In the early 1990s in the United Kingdom, the British Standards Institution (BSI) developed BS 7750, Environmental Management Systems, as a companion to its BS 5750 standard on quality management systems. BS 5750 was the forerunner and template for the ISO 9000 quality management standards. Countries participating in SAGE spent nearly two years studying BS 7750 and other national EMS standards to determine the need for an ISO international standard. The result of the study was the formation of ISO Technical Committee (TC) 207 and the beginning of the development of ISO 14001. In 1993, in the European Union, the European Commission adopted the Eco-Management and Audit Scheme (EMAS), which establishes, among other requirements, specifications for environmental management systems of companies doing business in the EU. National EMS standards become obsolete when ISO members accept ISO 14001 in their stead. In the United States, the U.S. Technical Advisory Group (TAG) to TC 207 has agreed to adopt ISO 14001 verbatim as the U.S. national standard with NSF International, the American Society for Testing and Materials (ASTM) and the American Society for Quality (ASQ) as co-sponsors.

4. What is TC 207?

Technical Committee (TC) 207 is the ISO group formed to develop a series of international environmental standards. Its official scope is "standardization in the field of environmental management tools and systems." TC 207 held its first plenary session in Toronto, Canada, in June 1993 and meets annually to review the progress of its subcommittees in developing standards in the ISO 14000 series.

5. What are EMAR and EMAS?

EMAR is the Eco-Management and Audit Regulation that contains the European Eco-Management and Audit Scheme (EMAS), which in turn establishes specifications for EMSs of companies with sites in the European Union (EU). EMAR was circulated first by the European Commission in draft form in December 1990 (before the publication of BS 7750). EMAR's initial intent was to require industries with the greatest propensity to pollute to register under the program and develop plans for continual improvement. EMAR has evolved to become an industry-specific process for voluntary evaluation and continual improvement of the environmental performance. EMAS is site-specific and voluntary. Companies in electronics, waste-management, aerospace and retail industries are only some of the industries experts predict will have to meet EMAS to maintain or increase their market shares. Theoretically, EMAS will not affect a U.S. company exporting goods, products or services without a European site. But according to experts, several European governments are likely to prefer doing business with EMAS-registered companies. EMAS-qualified sites must show evidence of a management system such as that contained in ISO 14001, as well as evidence of performance and auditing activities. It must issue a public statement of its objectives and targets, establish a register of significant environmental effects and pledge to use best available technologies, items not required in ISO 14001. The European Commission in Brussels, the EU's executive branch, evaluated four national standards for consideration as acceptable under EMAR. Besides BS 7750, the French, Spanish and Irish EMS standards were contenders for EMAR acceptance. All, with the exception of the French standard, were accepted by the EC as meeting EMAS requirements. The French Standard eventually was withdrawn as ISO 14001's acceptance became imminent. In September 1996, a group of EC experts agreed to recommend that the EC accept ISO 14001, with a "bridge" document, as meeting EMAS requirements. Final recognition occurred when ISO 14001 officially became published in September 1996.

6. What is the U.S. TAG?

The American National Standards Institute is the U.S. representative to ISO and to TC 207. It organized a U.S. Technical Advisory Group responsible for U.S. input on evolving environmental management documents reflecting U.S. interests. The U.S. TAG is broken down into Sub-Technical Advisory Groups (SubTAGs or STs); the sub-working group (SWG); and task groups (TGs) within the SubTAGs. Each of these groups has interest areas corresponding to TC 207 subcommittees and their working groups.

They help form a national consensus for content and application of the environmental standards for advocacy at the international level. No U.S. position is advocated unless a consensus has been developed in support of it. As of early 1997, there were more than 600 individuals representing some 300 organizations in the U.S. TAG, and this number continues to grow. Membership consists of representatives from government organizations, industry, consultants, registrars/auditors/standards bodies and public interest groups. The election of an EPA official to the vice-chair position in September 1995 indicates strong U.S. TAG interest in forging links between government and industry in the ISO 14000 area. The same EPA official has been re-elected and is serving in her second term.

    7. What is ISO 14001?

ISO 14001: Environmental Management Systems — Specification with Guidance for Use is the only "normative" standard in the series. It is the one against which a company's environmental management system will be audited — by an internal auditor or a third-party auditor — if a company chooses to have its EMS certified (registered). A company can self-declare. All the other standards in the ISO 14000 series are guidance or "informative" documents. ISO 14001 is a management system standard. It is not a performance or product standard, although the framers developed it with the idea that the result of its implementation should be better industry environmental performance. The standard represents a shift toward holistic proactive management and total employee involvement. ISO 14001 urges employees to define their environmental roles from the bottom up and requires top management backing, resources and visibility to support them. Comparable to the ISO 9001, 9002 and 9003 quality system specification standards, it is a comprehensive framework that contains core elements for managing a company's processes and activities to identify significant environmental aspects the organization can control and over which it can be expected to have an influence. The standard can be used by any company, facility or organization of any size in the world. While ISO 14001 likely is to be used in manufacturing or processing industries, it also can be applied to services such as construction, architecture, health care and engineering. This standard essentially requires a company to state what it does in environmental management and do what it states. ISO 14001 is not a product standard, is not an environmental performance standard, does not require you to establish or disclose performance levels or disclose audit results, does not require certification and is not required, period. The standard, developed by TC 207 SC1, was elevated to Draft International Standard status in July 1995 and published as a final standard in September 1996. ISO 14001 consists of the following sections/clauses:

1. Introduction. This section is a general orientation to the specification standard.
2. Scope. This is a statement that establishes the objectives of ISO 14001.
3. Normative References. This section states that there are no normative references, that is, there are no standards that are auditable that apply directly to this standard.
4. Definitions. This establishes definitions for the purpose of this standard, including definitions of an EMS, an EMS audit, an environmental aspect and continual improvement.
5. Environmental Management System Requirements. This follows the Plan-Do-Check-Act cycle, which companies must follow to ensure good EMS practice.

   Annex A (Informative) Guidance on the Use of the Specification. This annex is included to provide clarification in order to avoid any misinterpretation for self-declaration and/or third-party certification.

   Annex B (Informative) offers a chart illustrating the links between ISO 14001 and ISO 9001, showing where clauses in the two have largely congruent requirements.

   Annex C (Informative) contains bibliographical references to the ISO 9000 quality management and quality assurance standards, and to any ISO 14000 series document that exists at the time of publication.

8. What is the ISO 14004 guidance document?

ISO 14004: Environmental Management Systems — Guidelines on Principles, Systems and Supporting Techniques provides practical help on tailoring an EMS to a particular company. It sets forth EMS principles, explains fundamental environmental management concepts, defines key terms and offers a step-by-step walk-through of an EMS. It goes into more detail than does the ISO 14001 specification, combining the experience of the drafters in the practical application of an EMS. In particular, the guidance:

1. Establishes key principles for managers to use in implementing an EMS
2. Provides detail on all the steps needed to begin implementation
3. Suggests an implementation plan
4. Suggests a way a company may establish a system for measuring, monitoring and evaluating the performance of the management system against its objectives and targets
5. Suggests how a company should manage its continual improvement process

6. Offers examples of international environmental guiding principles

The drafters emphasized that the ISO 14004 document is not to be used for certification or to be audited against by auditors. It is for use by companies for internal guidance. The ISO 14004 document, developed by TC 207 SC1, suggests that the process and results of the initial environmental review should be documented. ISO 14004 was published, along with ISO 14001, as an international standard in September 1996.

9. What are the ISO 14020 labeling standards?

These standards are being developed by TC 207 SC3. ISO 14020: Environmental Labeling — General Principles is a standard to be used in the drafting process of all the labeling standards. It provides general principles to guide the development of specific environmental claims. ISO 14021: Terms and Definitions for Self-Declaration Environmental Claims establishes general guidelines regarding environmental claims in relation to the supply of goods and services. The objective of the standard in its draft form is to contribute to a reduction in the environmental burdens and impacts associated with the consumption of goods and services and to harmonize the use of environmental claims. This document is closely aligned with U.S. Federal Trade Commission guidelines interpreting FTC policy, laws and cases that indicate how the FTC will enforce the law in the area of environmental labeling claims. ISO 14022: Environmental Labeling — Self-Declaration Environmental Claims — Symbols is intended as a standard to ensure that symbols used to denote such things as recyclability and recycled content are understood to mean the same thing universally. ISO 14023: Environmental Labeling — Self-Declaration Environmental Claims — Testing and Verification was scheduled for preliminary work beginning in 1996. ISO 14024: Environmental Labeling — Guiding Principles, Practices, and Criteria for Multiple Criteria — Based Practitioner Programmes (Type I) — Guide for Certification Procedures is a guide for practitioner programs such as Blue Angel, Nordic Swan and Green Seal. The standard provides criteria for practitioners to use when evaluating products and awarding labels to companies. The ISO 14024 standard states that "the practitioner shall maintain a publicly available list of products which are currently licensed to carry the label." More than 25 different national programs exist, and those programs have the potential to create trade barriers throughout the world. However, the draft of the ISO 14024 eco-labeling document reflects many of the acceptable conditions that ISO members expect in a standard of this type. ISO 14025 Environmental Labels and Declarations Environmental Information Profiles — Type III Guiding Principles and Procedures is a labeling program resembling programs for nutritional labels placed on food products. As of early 1997, there were three types of labels:

1. Type I: third-party certified environmental labeling (subject of ISO 14024)
2. Type II: informative self-declaration claims (A Type II labeling proposal allowing an organization to issue a single symbol demonstrating conformance to ISO 14021 was removed from the SC3 work agenda at the June 1996 TC meeting in Rio de Janeiro, Brazil. Generally, Type II labeling refers to an organization's making self-declared environmental claims.)
3. Type III: quantified product information based on independent verification using indices (subject of ISO 14025)

Some time after the development of the labeling standards began, ISO 14022 and ISO 14023 were incorporated into ISO 14021; therefore, they no longer exist as separate, freestanding documents.

10. What is the ISO 14031 environmental performance evaluation standard?

This standard is being developed by TC 207 SC4. ISO 14031: Evaluation of Environmental Performance is the standard intended to define environmental performance evaluation (EPE) of management and operational systems of companies, and to provide guidance for adopting such a process. It includes examples of environmental preference indicators. EPE, in the context of an EMS, can be used both as a measurement/evaluation system and as a system for setting strategy. This process differs from an environmental audit in that an EPE is an ongoing review process conducted by line people responsible for the organization's environmental performance, as opposed to an audit that is conducted at infrequent intervals by people independent of the audited function.

11. What are the ISO 14040 life-cycle assessment standards?

Members of TC 207 SC5 are struggling to harness intricate concepts 20 years in the making and fraught with tangles. To complicate matters, the four standards they hope will help companies identify opportunities to reduce the environmental burdens of industrial processes must be practical, useful and economical. This is a struggle to analyze and predict the behavior of complex systems where scientific data, if available, are difficult to analyze in context of an LCA. ISO 14040: Environmental Management — Life-Cycle Assessment — Principles and Guidelines is a standard aimed at encouraging public policymakers, private organizations, and the public to approach environmental issues in a systematic manner that takes into account the environmental impact of a broader range of activities than has traditionally been the case. This standard is intended to be capable of being integrated into the operations of an organization and is not limited to application by third-party practitioners. ISO 14041: Environmental Management — Life-Cycle Assessment — Goal and Definition/Scope and Inventory Analysis is a standard seeking to give people directly involved in LCAs specific guidelines and requirements to help them formulate the goal and scope of a life-cycle assessment and inventory analysis. It concentrates on the LCA study's scope and on the process to conduct an inventory analysis such as defining the systems to be studied, the required input and output data, intended uses of the results, intended audience, the critical review process and the LCA's limitations, among other things. ISO 14042: Environmental Management — Life-Cycle Assessment — Impact Assessment is a standard proposing three major categories that should be considered in an impact assessment component of an LCA: classification, characterization, and valuation. ISO 14043: Environmental Management — Life-Cycle Assessment — Interpretation is a work in progress. In summer 1996, case studies were being reviewed for rough draft. The title of this standard was changed from LCA — Improvement Assessment because it was confusing to delegates.

12. What is the relationship between ISO 14000 and ISO 9000?
The common belief among professionals in the international standards arena is that the ISO 14000 EMS and auditing standards, and the ISO 9000 series of quality system standards ultimately should be aligned in some manner. A drive toward more efficient auditing will spur efforts to eliminate multiple audits, since there is a strong desire among industry members that there should only be one audit for management systems. In fact, in mid-1996, companies already were undergoing joint audits and at least one company received a joint ISO 90001/ISO 14001 certification. Integrating implementation of the standards at the operational level could help cut costs by making certification (registration) efforts more economical and audits less disruptive for auditees. Some of the language and concepts in ISO 14001 mirror those in ISO 9001, including a requirement for a policy statement, top management commitment, document control, training, corrective action, management review and continual improvement. However, there are several key differences, making ISO 14001 more demanding. ISO 14001 sections missing from ISO 9001 include specific policy requirements, environmental aspect identification, setting objectives and targets at all relevant levels, and the requirements that a company commit to complying with appropriate legislation and to prevention of pollution. As a result, ISO 14001 has legal implications missing from ISO 9000, and must take into account a broader array of stakeholders.

13. What is a certification body and what is certification?
Environmental management system certification is the result of an assessment and audit of an organization's environmental management system

by a third party, likely to be known as a certification body, or a "registrar" in U.S. terminology. The certification body evaluates an environmental management system of a facility site, portion of a site or group of similar sites, for conformity to ISO 14001. The evaluation will include an examination of the company's environmental policy, environmental management system and its documentation, EMS auditing pr ogram and procedures, and environmental records. It will include a thorough on-site audit to determine conformance to the ISO 14001 standard. Companies also can self-declare. Several countries adopted the ISO 14001 draft international standard as a national standard prior to ISO 14001's final adoption, and many companies became certified to the national standards and to the DIS version of ISO 14001. Once it became an international standard in September 1996, EU member nations accepted ISO 14001 as their single national standard. The seven steps of certification are:

1. Scope: A company or organization must identify the scope of the certification and the site to which it applies.
2. Application: All certification bodies (or registrars) require a completed application containing the rights and obligations from both the certification body and the client.
3. Document review: The certification body will ask the company or organization to submit documentation on its EMS.
4. Pre-assessment: Most registrars recommend a pre-assessment of the company or organization's current operating status; some require it.
5. Assessment: A full assessment is conducted to validate a site's readiness for ISO 14001 certification.
6. Certification: The three possible outcomes of an assessment are certification, conditional approval or disapproval.
7. Surveillance: Because an EMS is a living system, certificates must be renewed. Most certification bodies conduct surveillance every six to twelve months.

14. What's the difference among accreditation, certification and registration?

The following distinctions among the three terms are derived from the International Organization for Standardization's ISO/IEC Guide 2: General Terms and Their Definitions Concerning Standardization and Certification:

1. Certification is a procedure by which a third party gives written assurance that a product, process or service conforms to specified requirements. Certification to ISO 14001 stipulates that a company is in adherence with an environmental management system (EMS) that meets all requirements of ISO 14001.

2. Accreditation is a procedure by which an authoritative body gives formal recognition that a body or person is competent to carry out specific tasks. With regard to ISO 14001, accreditation means that a body is authorized to grant certification to a company that it has successfully assessed as meeting ISO 14001 EMS requirements and as having the processes in place to maintain that system.

3. Registration is a procedure by which a body indicates relevant characteristics of a product, process or service and then includes or registers the product, process or service in a publicly available list. In the United States, the term "registration" is used interchangeably with "certification" in the context of management system standard conformance and is not relevant to product registration. This can cause confusion. In Europe, environmental management systems "certification" is the proper term, rather than environmental management systems "registration," which is the U.S. terminology. The U.S. legal system denotes a degree of liability with the term "certification" that has been unacceptable to U.S. businesses, and hence the preference for using the term "registration."

15. How much does certification cost?

Experience with implementing ISO 14001 is limited, but indications are that the cost of certification varies according to the size of the company and the environmental system it has in place. Many U.S. companies at least have a rudimentary EMS in place, or many of the elements, but without the systems, which is likely to lower their costs. While comments from those with experience indicate the costs were expensive, most considered it worthwhile in terms of return on their investment. The average cost for a facility within a multi-national company such as 3M or Akzo Nobel averages about $100,000, while small and medium-sized companies are estimating between $50,000 and $75,000 per facility. There are many costs associated with certification, the first of which is actually developing and implementing the environmental management system. A company may elect to use only internal resources to implement the system, to rely completely on the services of an outside consultant or to combine both approaches. It is important to note that the cost-benefit ratio is going to depend entirely on individual circumstances. In one example of the benefits that might be derived, a major U.S. manufacturer saved $1 billion through an EMS approach over 20 years, and another major electronics company realized $32 million in 1990-91, according to an expert. In another case, the costs of implementing BS 7750 in one mid-sized British firm were about $17,600. The annual payback in efficiencies in energy, fuel, water, materials, and waste recycling was estimated at $23,000 (not including the benefits of improved customer and public relations).

16. How can I prepare for ISO 14000?

   1. Subscribe to voluntary initiatives on environmental management. Focus on current environmental management systems and work to improve them. Because there are many parallels between the two series, companies interested in preparing for the release of ISO 14001 should be familiar with ISO 9000.

   2. Design your environmental management system to conform to the ISO 14001 and integrate the system into your ISO 9000 framework as much as possible. You may need to perform a pre-audit assessment of your current EMS. This should help you avoid having to revise and rework your EMS.

   3. If you operate in or export to other countries, you may wish to conduct a country analysis to determine likely certification requirements. Likewise, an analysis of likely requirements of firms with which you do business may be in order.

   4. Develop an environmental auditing (EA) program or revise your present EA program, if necessary, to ensure that the auditors used by your organization meet the basic requirements of ISO 14012.

   5. Develop an internal process to evaluate your environmental performance and communicate that performance both inside and outside the company. Review the environmental labeling standard definitions as they are developed to ensure that your products and services are not at a disadvantage.

   6. Decide how you will integrate life-cycle thinking into management systems. Even after you develop your own life-cycle analysis standards, you should continually reexamine those methodologies and principles to avoid creating barrier-to-trade situations.

   7. Join the U.S. Technical Advisory Group to TC 207, or your country's equivalent, to keep abreast of developments or become involved in the standards' development as an expert. In the U.S., contact the American Society for Testing and Materials at (610) 832-9721.

   8. Keep an eye out for publications that are current and credible for continuous information and for help with assessing and implementing the standards.

   9. Surf the World Wide Web for information and sites to visit. You might begin with ISO's Web site: ISO Online.

10. Above all, remember that ISO 14001 — and other standards in the series — requires a holistic shift in thinking toward progressive environmental management at all levels of an organization. The benefits could be incalculable.

Index